Jump

MW01610696

Your _____, Vol VI

10 Inspiring Entrepreneurs Share Stories and Strategies on How to Jumpstart Many Areas of Your Life, Business, Mindset, and Success

Compiled by Katrina Sawa

CEO & Founder of JumpstartYourBizNow.com,
JumpstartPublishing.net and
13x Int'l Best-Selling Author

Jumpstart
PUBLISHING

Dear Susie
It's time to ignite
your client growth
engine! The sky's
the limit. Hugs,
Your Business Mentor,
Christine

Get to Know the 10 Inspiring Authors in this Book!

There's ONE page online where you can access all the authors' websites and special offers from this book to make it super easy for you to follow up and connect with them further.

Go to www.JumpstartBookAuthors.com right now before you forget. For a list of authors and their chapters, turn to the Table of Contents page.

Katrina Sawa, Speaker, 13x Int'l Best-Selling Author, Publisher, Award-Winning Business & Marketing Coach to Entrepreneurs Who Want More LOVE in Their Lives and MONEY in Their Businesses!

Published by K. Sawa Marketing International Inc. A.K.A. Jumpstart Publishing

P.O. Box 6, Roseville, CA 95661. (916) 872-4000
www.JumpstartPublishing.net

DISCLAIMER AND/OR LEGAL NOTICES

While all attempts have been made to verify information provided in this book and its ancillary materials, neither the authors nor publisher assume any responsibility for errors, inaccuracies, or omissions and are not responsible for any financial loss by customer in any manner. Any slights of people or organizations are unintentional. If advice concerning legal, financial, accounting, health or related matters is needed, the services of a qualified professional should be sought. This book and its associated ancillary materials, including verbal and written training, are not intended for use as a source of legal, financial or accounting advice.

EARNINGS & INCOME DISCLAIMER

With respect to the reliability, accuracy, timeliness, usefulness, adequacy, completeness, and/or suitability of information provided in this book, Katrina Sawa, K. Sawa Marketing International Inc., its partners, associates, affiliates, consultants, and/or presenters make no warranties, guarantees, representations, or claims of any kind. Readers' results will vary. This book and all products and services are for educational and informational purposes only. Katrina Sawa and/or K. Sawa Marketing International Inc. is not responsible for the success or failure of your business, personal, health or financial decisions relating to any information presented by Katrina Sawa, K. Sawa Marketing International Inc., or company products/services.

Any examples, stories, reference, or case studies are for illustrative purposes only and should not be interpreted as testimonies and/or examples of what readers and/or consumers can generally expect from the information.

ISBN: 978-1-7358666-5-9

PRINTED IN THE UNITED STATES OF AMERICA

Dedication

This book is dedicated to Entrepreneurs everywhere who have the desire and mission to make a bigger impact with those they serve.

Here's to creating and enjoying the business and life of your dreams!

Special thank you to my husband Jason and stepdaughter Riley who support me 100% on all of my entrepreneurial endeavors. And thank you to all of the awesome jumpstart authors that have written their stories and strategies in this and previous books.

Praise for the *Jumpstart Your _____* Books

These are my favorite books to read.

"This is the perfect time for this book to come out. I'm so glad I bought this! So many incredible stories of ways to jumpstart your business, your love life, your dreams, anything you can think of. These are my favorite books to read. I definitely recommend this book!" - Candi & Sean Douglas

Great read -- Short doses of inspiration

"This is a great book. Many tidbits of motivation. You can read any chapter and gain inspiration to take on the day's challenges. I love the stories and perspectives provided." - Karen T. Peak

Another great book by Katrina Sawa & Friends

"Katrina Sawa always brings her readers beneficial info for growing a business in the current marketplace." - PK Odle

Excellent Co-Authors with a variety of backgrounds

"Really great content, the authors here have a variety of backgrounds which is great for insight!" - Matt Brauning

A Great Source of Inspiration!

"Being an entrepreneur is a really tough... but rewarding job! Sometimes you need a little extra encouragement to push you through the rough times. This is an incredible book, packed with all kinds of inspiring entrepreneur stories. I found nuggets of wisdom and inspiration all at the same time!" - Richard B. Greene

Katrina Sawa Never Disappoints

"Katrina Sawa never disappoints when she is delivering information to her audience of fans, and she certainly delivers with her latest book. Thank you, Katrina, for gathering this group of experts to provide us with a great resource." - RL Escobar-Balcom

There is Something for Everyone!

"Jumpstart Your _____ is filled with powerful stories and insightful takeaways that can help you grow your business and more importantly, enjoy your life. There is something for everyone! Bottom line - this book ROCKS!" - Craig Duswalt, Keynote Speaker, Author, Podcaster, and Creator of Rock Your Life.

So much great Inspiration!

"Hard to believe so much great information is available in ONE book. Whatever you dream... you can achieve! You are bound to find something impactful in this book!" - Marguerite Crespillo

Creative and Inspiring

"This is one of the rare Kindle books I carved out time to read. Creative and inspiring – great ideas in multiple life areas, love this. Didn't know about this "jumpstart" series - going to check out Volumes 1-4 now to see what else I'm missing." – Doc Champagne

Realistic Strategies

"This is a must-read if you are looking for inspiration, realistic strategies or just a reason not to give up. These women and the stories of what they have done in their businesses can give you that. So glad that I made this book purchase." – Samantha M.

Inspiring and Motivating Book

"Each author wrote of relevant information. Every woman I know could benefit from reading this book. I truly enjoyed reading this." – Melanie (Amazon purchaser)

TABLE OF CONTENTS

This book is divided first by topics relating to jumpstarting one's life and self, then by business-oriented chapters. Within each section, chapters are categorized alphabetically.

JUMPSTART RESOURCES

Introduction

This book, *Jumpstart Your _____, Volume VI*, is for you if you need a jumpstart in any area of your life, career, business, mindset, health, relationships, prosperity, beliefs, and more!

This is the sixth book in the *Jumpstart Your _____* series, and we keep getting new, fresh topics, content, and authors! This volume has 9 new authors in addition to myself. We have a wide variety of chapters, with advice for the business owner, woman, man, professional, speaker, parent, as well as the person who wants to improve his or her life, career, health, and even relationship with themselves and/or significant other. It's fun to see who comes through with each book, and what expertise they bring.

The authors with whom I have collaborated on this book are experts in their industries and in what they teach. Our goal is to provide a book that shows you how and why you should consider jumpstarting many of the areas covered within these chapters.

If you enjoy any one or more of the stories and chapters within this book, please reach out and contact the author(s). They want to know that their chapter encouraged you, inspired you, or motivated you in some way. They also want to know how they can help you. Each author has provided some kind of next step or free gift at the end of their chapter, to give you the opportunity to learn more. Don't stop with this book: please take the initiative and reach out for more information, more help, and more advice for whatever you might be trying to jumpstart in your life right now. Who knows maybe after your initial read-through of this book, you will pick it up a couple years from now and decide to jumpstart something else!

This edition of *Jumpstart Your* ____ can help literally anyone, I believe. There are chapters you'll find immediately helpful, and some you may not need until years from now--but keep it handy just in case, because you never know!

Half of the chapters in this book will help you jumpstart an area of your personal life, and half of them are geared more towards helping business owners. Whether or not you have a business, one day you may! Order extra copies of these books for friends, family, or clients; they will appreciate your thoughtfulness.

What about you? Do you have an area of expertise about which you could write in one of our *Jumpstart Your* ____ books? One thing I know to be true is that

Introduction

most entrepreneurs really do need a book in this day and age. You need to be an author to really be seen as the expert in your industry, or even in the company for which you work. Writing a whole book by yourself is a lot of work, takes a lot of time, and sometimes costs a lot of money. Being an author in a compilation book like this one, however, is a lot less cumbersome, less stressful, and less costly. It's also helpful when somebody puts it all together for you, and you don't have to worry about all the details of editing, cover design, proofing, and publishing. (That's what we do here at Jumpstart Publishing.)

I've been in business since 2002. I've been an author in now 19 compilation books, plus three of my own full-length books. I have put together this opportunity to become a published author, with very little effort and work on your part--if you're interested. Contact me if you might be interested in being an author in the next *Jumpstart Your* _____ book and share your story! Go to www.JumpstartPublishing.net for details.

And if you've ever thought about starting, growing, or marketing your own business, and/or becoming an author or speaker, please reach out to me; I'm extremely passionate about helping anybody build a profitable business doing what they love. - Katrina Sawa

Jumpstart Your Life/Self Chapters

Jumpstart Your Empowered Self

3 Keys to Getting What You Really Want

By Christi Cossette

Putting yourself first goes against what women are taught. We are natural nurturers who are focused on caring for those around us, always putting others' needs before our own. We are told to shrink back, be small, don't take up too much room. Don't be too loud, too thin, too fat, too tall, too short, and the list goes on. It seems it's impossible to ever be good enough to meet society's standards—especially because they keep changing.

If you spend your life bowing to the opinions, needs, and desires of everyone else, you risk losing yourself in the process, never reaching your God-given potential. Perhaps worst of all, you don't serve anyone in your life or family well, because you're too exhausted and confused to do anything well. Does this sound familiar?

I've been there. From a young age, I was taught there were very clear roles that a woman must play versus a man. Both of my parents worked, but my mom also carried the load of child rearing, shopped for food, clothes, and other necessities, ensured we had everything we needed, got us to school on time, made sure we received proper nutrition and exercise, and took us to the doctor as needed. Once I had children of my own, I did my best to keep all the balls in the air. I worked full-time and struggled to balance my responsibilities at work and home. While at work, I felt guilty for being gone and letting someone else "raise my children," but when I was home, I worried that I wasn't doing enough at work to be successful. Each time I had a child, I was put into an invisible "penalty box," and my career was put on hold for a minimum of a year each time. As soon as I told my boss I was expecting, regardless of whether they were male or female, I always received the same responses:

"You need to focus on your family now; I'll give your big projects to someone else so you can take it easy."

"I'll send someone else on that business trip, since they don't have children."

"We don't want to put you on any big projects since you'll be gone for months, and we need someone who can carry the project through."

"Just enjoy this time to relax."

I'd give in, largely because I was so tired during my pregnancies, and it wasn't worth the fight. Then, when I came back from leave, it was a slow onboarding to assign projects to me so I could "ease back into things." They didn't want to give me too much too soon. Sounds great on the surface, but meanwhile, my colleagues were given key opportunities while I took a back seat. After having three children, I found myself years behind in my career.

What I didn't know at the time was that, with each pregnancy, my hormones got more and more out of balance. And the more I invested in my kids and husband, the less time I had for myself. I felt as though I was failing at everything. I was being pulled in so many directions that I wasn't doing anything well. I was too tired to play with my kids. I didn't have time to cook healthy meals, so we ate out a lot, which made us all tired and cranky due to the lack of nutrition. I started gaining weight. I was anxious and irritable. I often snapped at my husband and kids for simple things, because I was so overloaded that any small request seemed like a monumental task. Couldn't they see how tired I was? Didn't they know how hard I was working? How could they possibly need MORE than what I was already giving?

I soon realized something had to change. But what could I do? I enjoyed working, and I also needed the money, so quitting my job wasn't an option. I loved my family and wanted to spend as much time with them as possible, but I noticed that our time together wasn't very fun or meaningful. We weren't making memories and sharing special moments together like I'd imagined. Instead, "frazzled" me would try to take them somewhere fun, only to freak out when my toddler spilled something, someone threw a tantrum, or I forgot something at home.

I wanted quality time with my family, not just quantity of time. I started reaching out to female mentors to see how they "did it all." I listened to books and podcasts on work/life balance and was drawn to topics on health and how to restore your energy. I quickly learned that these mentors DIDN'T do it all! Instead, they had learned several key secrets to managing their daily lives while prioritizing themselves and what mattered most to them.

I started learning and applying these secrets, and now I have a wonderful, thriving marriage, a happy home life with our three kids, a wonderful corporate career in senior leadership that I enjoy, and I live in a home I love, in a great neighborhood with supportive friends and neighbors. We have the freedom to take regular vacations, drive cars that feel both functional and luxurious, and we can pay for small luxuries like a house cleaner, a nanny, and monthly massages.

Do I have it ALL today? It depends on who you're asking, but to me, my deepest wishes have come true. And I'm ONLY 42. I used to think it could never come fast enough, and now that I've built a life I love, I've realized that I have decades ahead of me, God willing, to continue growing, learning, and loving. YOU, too, can build a life you love!

Here are 3 key secrets to start applying in your life, and you'll soon watch the changes take shape into a beautiful future that becomes today.

Secret #1: Work / life balance is an illusion. Focus on adaptability instead.

I had always wanted both a family and a career. I knew I wanted to be in senior level leadership one day. Yet, I saw all these men and women killing themselves to get ahead at work, barely seeing their families, some on their second or third marriages. I didn't want that for myself. Was it possible to continue growing in my career without giving my husband and kids a backseat? The short answer is YES!

To truly achieve and maintain the joy, peace, and balance you want in your life, the first secret is

ADAPTABILITY! The truth is that work/life balance is a myth. The reality is that, instead of daily ongoing balance, your life ebbs and flows. The more you can shift your focus to what matters most at that time, the more personal satisfaction you will find. Rather than striving for balance in life, you should instead strive for adaptability: focus on what matters each day as your needs and priorities change.

Secret #2: You must learn to put yourself FIRST!

We can't pour from an empty cup. You need to ensure you are taking care of yourself in whatever way works best for you. You need 7-8 hours of sleep, proper nutrition, daily movement, and a focus on stress management. If you focus on supporting your energy and putting yourself FIRST, you can be the best version of yourself and build a life you love that supports both you and your family, while simultaneously thriving at work.

I learned to ask for help when I needed it. I developed morning and evening routines to support my needs. I started taking walks in the middle of the day while at work to clear my head and refresh myself. I got enough sleep to support my body, and I started changing how I ate. I also learned that I am an introvert and need alone time to recharge. This meant I had to schedule time away from my family so when I was with them, I'd be the best version of myself instead of the tired, cranky zombie I'd become.

I learned to delegate tasks I don't enjoy such as cooking and cleaning, and I set boundaries around my work schedule so when I am done for the day, I am completely done and can close that window in my brain and focus on my family. My husband and I also started prioritizing our marriage, and we go on dates at least every other week so we stay connected. The best thing we can do for our boys is to model a healthy relationship, so they feel stable and secure knowing their parents love each other.

Secret #3: Align your time (your calendar), your finances, and your daily HABITS to your priorities.

This will require BOUNDARIES and learning to say no! All of the above sounds nice, but if you don't make a plan, block time in your calendar for what matters most, or budget for what fills your cup, you are setting yourself up to fail. Consistency truly matters here. What you do every day becomes a habit you no longer need to think about, and then it becomes easy.

This may seem overwhelming, but you have what it takes! You can do this too! As a Women's Empowered Action Coach, I work with clients to build confidence, take focused action, find balance, and crush their goals! I can help YOU make time for what is important while having the impact you desire on the world! Stop settling for second best when it comes to your career, your relationships, and your wellbeing. Whether you are an executive, run your own business, or have a J-O-B... don't settle for the things you don't like, or which no longer serve you. Be empowered to take action! All forward progress comes down to your daily decisions...moment to moment to moment. You are one decision away from changing your life! Your choices are truly that powerful! All you have to do is change your mind, and then act accordingly.

If you feel empowered to put yourself first and get what you really want, but you aren't sure how to get there, I'd love to have a conversation with you.

I also have a quiz to help you figure out what's missing, identify what you want, and dive deeper to get to the heart of where you're stuck...you may not see it. These tools will help you self-assess where you are and figure out a plan to go after what you really want. It's about taking enough of the right actions toward your goal, believing it's possible, and having the right guidance along the way.

And finally, you can get my free download, "20 Rules to Live By," as well as a free audio on how to put yourself first. You can find all these tools and more at www.ChristiCossette.com/jumpstart.

By Christi Cossette

I want to end with a part of my very favorite quote by Marianne Williamson, from her book *A Return to Love*:

"Our deepest fear is not that we are inadequate. Our deepest fear is that we are powerful beyond measure. It is our light, not our darkness, that most frightens us. We ask ourselves, 'Who am I to be brilliant, gorgeous, talented, fabulous?' Actually, who are you not to be? You are a child of God. Your playing small does not serve the world."

About Christi Cossette

Christi is a wife, mother, corporate executive, strategic and transformational leader, and a Women's Empowered Action Coach who specializes in confidence, focused action, finding balance, and goal achievement. She is passionate about supporting women leaders as they work to climb the corporate ladder, grow their businesses, build their teams, and expand their influence while simultaneously managing their home lives and physical and mental health, so they can make time for what is important.

Jumpstart Your Focus

The Power of Prioritized Productivity

By Katrina Sawa

I want you to be ridiculously successful in whatever venture you choose. This means that you'll probably need to learn some new skills along the way. You definitely need to become a better speaker and a knowledgeable businessperson if you run your own business. You will want to become a better leader and an influencer if you plan to do big things in life, in your career, or even as the leader of your own family.

So, what does it take?

It takes FOCUS.

When I first started my business back in 2002, I focused on attending as many local networking events in person as I could every month, as I knew it would take dozens and dozens of connections to secure enough clients to support the income level I wanted to achieve.

Furthermore, I had a kick-butt, proven follow-up system that I used to book appointments and get clients. I was very assertive and consistent, and I got results.

My system worked to a certain extent to build a reasonably successful business, but I wanted more.

I sought out workshops and mentors to gain as much knowledge as I could in the areas that would help me grow and attain a more consistently profitable business doing what I loved. I learned a lot, and I kept learning, year after year. I grew my business to 6 figures and beyond, and I'm so grateful and thankful for everyone who played a part in teaching me what I didn't know I didn't know.

Looking back on it now, 21 years from that first day, I recognize what it was that has allowed me the success, income, clients, and happiness that I have since achieved on a consistent basis.

It was my confident sense of awareness and commitment to the end result, along with the unwavering, persistent actions I took, that got me to where I am today. In a roundabout way, I call this FOCUS.

Entrepreneurs especially need to have focus, or we tend to get sidetracked by our own creative minds and with the numerous distractions going on outside ourselves. I know this firsthand, as I'm constantly coming up with creative ideas to grow and scale my business (and my clients' businesses). I've learned to prioritize my ideas and not to act on them in the very moment they come. That can definitely throw off your focus.

I call this your **"Order of Importance."** Depending on where you are in your business, you could have a different "Order of Importance" than another entrepreneur—so definitely don't compare yourself to others. For example, if you're newer in business or you're still focused on building consistent revenue, then you will be more focused on Revenue-Generating Activities on a daily basis. If you're a more seasoned entrepreneur, then you are most likely focused on scaling, leveraging, and outsourcing. Wherever you are in your business, the power of Focus is critical to your success.

Being extremely productive, organized, and efficient is how I get so much done. It's how I have multiple projects going at any given time. It's how I manage 20-35 clients on a monthly basis, all with full access to me. It's the reason why some clients call me the Energizer Bunny and are in awe of how much I get done and participate in. It's how I don't lose sight of what's most important: my family and myself. And, it's how my family and I can take two (or more) long vacations every year and multiple three-to-four-day getaways.

Being organized with your:

- To Dos
- Inboxes
- Computer Documents and Files
- Paper
- Home
- Office
- Household
- Finances
- Marketing
- Systems
- Team

... can lead to more success in your life as well!

In fact, this year, my word for the year wasn't a word; it was a phrase: "Focus on What Matters."

I created an online Summit and Giveaway on that topic. I wrote articles and blogs on that topic. I scheduled my time around things that mattered to me the most. I made decisions to take on projects or travel to events based on whether they would serve my higher good, keeping my focus on what mattered to me this year.

My stepdaughter is entering into high school this fall, starting to really explore her options and learn more about herself, and I want to be there to support her. My husband and I are beginning a journey into real estate investing, and I want to devote some time to learning and growing in that field. We adopted a new dog at the beginning of the year who has brought huge amounts of love into our home, and we're all enjoying that. And finally, my mom is struggling with lung cancer this year, so I'm leaving space for her when she needs me.

There are a lot of things on *your* plate too, I'm sure, areas on which *you* want to be more focused—and I'm sure if you freed up more of your time (either with work or your business), you would have more time for what matters to you. This is why I'm so passionate about this topic. I see too many people *not* living their best or happiest lives, and I want so badly for everyone to have the opportunity to do so. These people aren't making enough of the *right* things a priority, or else they aren't getting the support to see what else they can do to transform certain areas for more ease or profit.

Setting boundaries is another part of being more focused. For many people, it's not easy saying "NO" to someone, especially a client or a referral partner.

I've learned this lesson the hard way, but now I pace myself throughout the year with joint ventures, promotions, and projects. I have boundaries for when I'm available and when I'm not, and I put MY TIME on my calendar first, so I know I have enough time to complete the things I need to get done DURING business hours. I don't postpone my own needs until "after hours" anymore; instead, I focus on my clients during the allotted time in which I choose to work—no matter the time of day or evening. This way, I can be sure I am not pushing my most important priorities out of the way to make room for work.

Another aspect of getting and staying more focused is the ability to be more **productive**, moving through tasks and making decisions swiftly. The longer it takes you to make decisions, the more stagnant you can become.

"Money follows speed," I once heard a speaker say at a conference, and I've lived by that motto ever since.

You may be thinking, "Katrina, I don't feel like any of what you're saying here comes naturally to me. I know I need to focus more so I can maximize my time, but it really comes hard to me."

I would say that there are certain personality characteristics that make it easier for some people to focus than others, but focusing can also be a learned skill. You can practice and have accountability partners to help you stay focused; it doesn't all have to rely on you.

An article published by the US Chamber of Commerce on December 8, 2020, revealed the **Top 6 Personality Traits of Successful Entrepreneurs** (I added the remarks), which are:

1. Persuasiveness - Oh yes, that helps with the marketing and sales aspects of the job!

2. Flexibility - But of course! We certainly have no control over whether our technology will work or not, right? Or if a phenomenon like Covid hits...we just have to pivot!

3. Creativity - That's what keeps us up at night with the next big idea!

4. Self-Motivation - This is where the ability to stay focused comes in really handy so we can get more done in less time or with less effort.

5. Tenacity – This is yet another trait to help you hold yourself accountable and become more driven and unstoppable.

6. Passion – Sure! If you're not passionate about what you're doing, you're doing the wrong thing.

Where do you lie with those 6 traits? They pretty much describe me to a T.

If they don't automatically describe you, never fear. You'll find your way to getting and staying more focused while remaining creative, flexible, and fulfilled. And, as I mentioned before, you don't have to be an entrepreneur to find these tips helpful.

I wasn't always this focused. I think I had short-term focus back in school. I was really good at taking and passing tests with flying colors, but I did not remember much of what I studied. I would cram for my tests the night before, focusing on the most important aspects of what I thought I needed to know, then I'd take the test. Not a day later, I couldn't remember hardly any of the information I'd been taught. Cramming isn't the best solution, mind you, especially if you need to retain a lot of information for your profession, such as a doctor or an attorney would.

Here's my take on what you need to do in order to become more focused.

FOCUS stands for:

Fearless - You are fearless when you lean into your biggest fear and act towards it—you make fear your friend, not your enemy. Once you overcome that resistance, once you face that fear and embrace it, every other fear in your world becomes irrelevant.

Becoming more fearless will allow you to keep an open mind to what else is possible. It will help you continue to move forward when doubts creep in. It will help you stay focused on what matters most, and in the entrepreneurial world, that means revenue-generating activities almost 100% of the time.

Observant - You are observant when you have a heightened sense of awareness. You notice everything very quickly, and keep a sharp eye on your surroundings and what's going on.

Becoming more observant will allow you to stay mindful of what's important, attentive to what needs to get done (or done first), and away from distraction by bright, shiny objects, or "Squirrels!"

Committed - A committed person is simply one who regularly keeps their commitments, what he or she has signed up to do or not to do. They are dedicated to doing whatever it takes to see the action through to the end result. They are passionate and zealous about their beliefs and desires.

Becoming more committed will allow you to let your passion shine through and keep you marching forward towards your goals, whether big or small.

Unwavering - An unwavering person is one who continues in a strong and steady way. They have steadfast faith and determination. They are firm, unshakable, and will stay on point.

Becoming more unwavering will allow you to remain consistent with your actions and to be less waffling when it comes to decision making.

Strong-minded - You are strong-minded when you are more purposeful, sure, and self-disciplined. Strong-minded is not necessarily opinionated or dominant, although it can sound as such.

Becoming more strong-minded will help you become more determined, strong-willed, and persistent, which is the key to getting what you want.

Hopefully, you have more ideas about how to use these thoughts to become more Focused in your life and your business.

I would love to invite you to visit my website to experience more of what I have to offer, including some free trainings, videos, and downloads. I've put together a page just for those of you reading this chapter to get to know me better and learn some valuable tips to support you in your growth. Come on over and let's connect on a deeper level. Visit www.JumpstartYourFocus.com today, and I'll see you soon!

About Katrina Sawa

Katrina is an International Award-Winning Speaker and Author with 22 books. Entrepreneurs hire her to learn exactly what to do and how to grow their businesses quickly. Katrina is passionate about finding the holes and opportunities for business owners to monetize and systematize so they can work less and make more. Katrina hosts numerous trainings, mastermind retreats, summits, and one-on-one coaching to help others get a jumpstart—fast!

Jumpstart Your Health

Our Emotional, Physical, and Spiritual Journey

By Shuree Wesley

As a child, and later as a young woman, I experienced and witnessed multiple tragedies. I have been a victim of sexual assault, witnessed another person become a victim of sexual assault, had a boyfriend hold a gun to my head, had my home robbed by drug addicts, watched my mother endure abuse and marry a man who went to prison for rape, and witnessed a police raid of my home when I was just a small child. The tragedy that almost broke my soul was having to watch one of my children battle alcoholism, depression, and suicidal thoughts. As a mom, you're never prepared for such an experience. It led to me and my husband making the devastating decision to let our child experience homelessness.

Although our child, who is a grown adult now, is no longer homeless, I watch daily as they regain the strength to overcome their inner demons.

I never felt wanted or loved when I was younger, due to my mother's ongoing emotional abuse and neglect. I felt like she hated me. She claimed my father had abused her, which left me feeling confused and responsible for her pain. For years I felt conflicted: I was responsible for the safety of my little brother, I loved him very much and did not want him to feel abandoned—yet I so badly wanted to get out.

At the age of 16, I gave birth to my daughter. Although I was briefly married, I realized he was not the right person for me at such a young age. He seemed burdened by his own pain, and I often felt its reflection in the way he treated me. Eventually, he had an affair, and we split up. Once again, I was left with the old feelings of betrayal, isolation, and unworthiness. In my heart, I knew this was not what I deserved, and it was not my fault.

As I grew into a young woman, I became very aware of my surroundings and paid close attention to people and their behaviors. I felt like a mother bear and a lion all in one, always on the lookout to keep my daughter safe, sensing old energy and protecting us. I wanted to be the best mother I could be for her, so I immersed myself in studying health as a hobby. I became obsessed with understanding it. I exercised regularly, studied holistic care, and made sure we practiced clean eating. We attended church to nourish our souls. Life had much more in store for us, and the best was yet to come.

Health became a significant aspect of my life. I dedicated myself to regular nutrition, exercise, and physical education, finding solace in the company of like-minded people. I prioritized healthy eating, exercise, nutrition, and teaching nutrition.

I always noticed my body's reaction to the energy I felt inside whenever I was around health-minded people, and I listened to my intuition. I went to college. I enjoyed learning about human behavior, the effects of trauma, and the brain injuries it causes. It was such an inspirational time in my life. The positive effects were endless. My confidence changed.

Health began to overflow into all aspects of my life. First, I focused on nutrition. It was followed by emotional, physical, and spiritual wellbeing, as I strove to become the healthiest version of myself. Embracing self-love and gratitude has been instrumental in this journey.

The reason I want to talk about jumpstarting your health in this chapter is not just because my husband, brother, and daughter have opened two health stores and a gym we named Lion's Den—but it's because I truly believe, having gone through even more trauma and chaos in my life, that how we live our lives matters more than we think.

Our Emotional Health is how we handle adversity, how resilient we become, how we love ourselves fully, and how we project all of that into society—but most of all, it is how we lead and guide our families.

Our Physical Health is critical for sustaining a long, well-lived life full of beautiful and meaningful experiences, overcoming challenges, and setting good examples for our loved ones.

Our Spiritual Health consists of our beliefs, values, feelings of belonging, and our inner being. Without a higher power for guidance, who will you trust, believe in, or look up to?

My hope is that you're hearing about my journey, my struggles, and how I have been so fortunate to survive and overcome—and that you are beginning to recognize within your own journey how you think, feel, believe, and act in order to overcome your biggest setbacks and challenges.

Because I'm such a physical health-conscious person, I recall going to restaurants as a child and observing what food choices families made. I noticed the commonalities between smiles, weight, clothing they wore, and so on. I remember how much happiness I felt whenever I raced other classmates on the playground, and I was often the fastest girl in my class (and normally a runner-up with the boys). How elated it made me feel inside! How proud my teachers and others in my school were of me! I always smile and feel the energy in my body reacting positively to these memories. I knew back then (and fully believe now) that we have to embrace our bodies; after all, we're each given only one.

15 years ago, I married the man of my dreams: my soulmate. He is the man who accepted, understood, loved, and made me feel safe. This man was everything I had ever wanted. I never felt judged, nor did he ever question my past. He did not need to. He never cared about where I came from. He admired who I had become. He was grateful for me, and I was grateful for him. He loved me fiercely.

We purchased our dream home on the cliffside with breathtaking views of sunrises and sunsets. Years later, we witnessed the strength, bravery, and loyalty of our family as we united to overcome the unimaginable.

My husband is a Board-Certified Master Arborist. He worked on several fires in the past, but this one felt different. We had built a great business together over the years.

Sensing that something was not right about the fire, he called with alarming concern. As the flames drew closer to the town of Paradise, he knew he had to act swiftly to ensure the safety of our daughter, Aundrea, and our grandson. My husband's persistence saved their lives. Having witnessed the fiery destruction that had already claimed their neighbors' homes, Aundrea grabbed her baby and her dog, leaving everything else behind.

In that moment, my heart sank: my husband was driving into the fire to ensure his daughter's safety, and my daughter was driving through the fire to ensure her son's safety.

I waited helplessly; I had no control over the outcome of my family's safe return. I felt empty, guilty, and ashamed that I was not there to help. I believed in them and had faith they would make it.

It was slow, bumper-to-bumper traffic as my brother walked onto our property. He arrived just in time to see the fire taking our home.

My youngest daughter was on the phone with me, keeping me calm. She will never understand the comfort she provided me that day, simply by reassuring me that she was on her way to help us. The feeling of a family coming together is all I had ever wished for as a little girl.

Aundrea was a new mom at the time, and she became her son's guardian angel: she protected and saved her baby boy. Today is July 21st, as I write this. It is his 6th birthday. Thank you, God, for protecting my entire family that day, for showing me the power of love and rewarding me with this family.

My brother will never understand how much I love him for his incredible loyalty that day. He was brave. He showed his family that, no matter what, he would be there to take care of us all, even if he had to walk through fire with his cousins.

My husband proved himself to be the protector I had always been determined to find. He will never understand how it makes a woman feel to know a man will drive through fire for her children. He is my hero. My soulmate, my forever love. My destiny.

I felt the Power of Love and Gratitude in the midst of the chaos, as love and strength radiated from everyone around me. Bumper-to-bumper traffic filled the road, with each passing car serving as a reminder of the countless lives affected by the wildfire. Despite the uncertainty and fear, I felt overwhelming gratitude for the presence of my family and their unwavering support. This was no ordinary fire—it was a catastrophic force of nature, akin to an atomic bomb.

The wildfire brought our family together like never before, revealing the depth of our love, loyalty, and courage. We may have lost our home, but we gained an unbreakable bond that reaffirmed the power of family and faith. Despite the hardships, our united front and unwavering determination allowed us to overcome yet another tragedy. The experience highlighted the heart of lions that beat within each one of us, forever connected by the unbreakable thread of love.

After years of recovery from the fire, after COVID, we were guided into our passion of opening those health stores and the gym I previously mentioned. We were focused and excited once again. We built a new home, even better than the other one.

This year still brought much loss, however; we said goodbye to my mom in April and my grandmother soon after that. My grandmother was the one who never gave up on me.

I have focused on family, healing my soul, and loving myself. I recognize that overall health encompasses emotional, physical, and spiritual well-being. Emotional health, in particular, is crucial, as it can affect one's self-worth. My childhood experiences taught me to protect myself from emotional abuse and to be vigilant about the people with whom I surround myself.

I am thankful for the inspiration my husband and I provide to others, and I know that I am making a positive difference in this world.

If you're interested in connecting with me, I would love to connect with you! I choose to surround myself with those who are on a similar journey to me, those who want to improve their emotional, physical, and spiritual health and who are ready to do whatever it takes to continue seeking out their best selves. I provide meal planning, coaching, and physical training.

I want to gift you something very special. It's a nutrition plan, and it will help you focus on the direction you can take to improve your health. Please reach out to me at shuree@nutrishopchico.com if you want some support to make jumpstarting your health a little easier and more fulfilling.

About Shuree Wesley

Shuree Wesley, a beacon of accomplishment, shines across diverse realms. A luminary in coaching, nutrition, authorship, investment, and entrepreneurship, her impact radiates from Northern California. Guiding an Arborist enterprise for 15 years, she soared to six-figure success via strategic marketing. Shuree orchestrates thriving nutrition stores, a gym, and another Arborist victory. Media features highlight her wisdom on growth and crisis management. An inspiration, she propels entrepreneurs to exceed boundaries, achieving remarkable grandeur.

Jumpstart Your Love Life

Making Love a Priority

By Katrina Sawa

Six and a half years into my "starter marriage," I realized my husband was no longer supportive of me and the fact that I had chosen to become an entrepreneur. When I quit my last JOB and decided to build my own business, he became fearful that I wouldn't bring in a steady paycheck anymore. He would say things to me that hurt very much, such as: "Maybe you should just go back and get a job."

I would go to networking events—something I usually loved to do—and I'd put a big smile on my face, tell everyone that everything was ok, then cry myself to sleep at night because I felt like I wasn't loved or supported. I spent two years like that, trying to make him understand my new goals and aspirations. He didn't have any interest in knowing what my new career entailed, or in understanding me and how my needs and desires had changed.

I don't want you to be in a situation like this. It hurts not to be supported in what you really want to do or be. I wasn't willing to settle any longer, and I hope you aren't either. I was 35 years old at the time. I asked myself, "Do I want to live like this for the next 40-50 years?" The answer was "NO," so I left that marriage.

It was just a little over two years into starting my business, and I hadn't created consistent cash flow. What I did have was FAITH. I had faith in myself, that it would all work out. I had faith in myself that I knew what I was doing, I was good at it, and people needed me. And I was determined to succeed because I was no longer interested in going back to a JOB.

What I realized, however, after a few relationship workshops, was that I had played a part in the marriage going awry—just as I had played a part with some of my interim relationships that didn't work out in between my "starter marriage" and my "keeper marriage," the one I'm in now. I learned I was emasculating the men I was with. It's a hard pill to swallow and an even harder one to admit here, but if I can improve and change, so can you (if you need to). I write a lot about the changes I've made in my book, *Love Yourself Successful.*

I think we always have to continue improving ourselves, our mindsets, our personal relationships, and our businesses. There is always more to learn, as well as better ways to be.

I used to think I was "good." It was them, not me. But I no longer think so. In fact, I feel so blessed to have found my current husband who makes me want to continue to learn how to be a better person, wife, communicator, and friend.

Where YOU come in.

A few years after my divorce, I started wondering why about 60 percent of my business coaching clients wouldn't do what I told them to do with their marketing in order to get more clients. It was simple, I thought. I had laid it all out for them: where to go, what to say, what to do, how to market and sell, etc. But they wouldn't do it, or else they always had an excuse not to take action.

I started asking some of them, "How's your love life?"

We'd get into the conversation about their significant other, whether they were married, dating, or single. I began asking all my clients about their love relationships. I wanted to find out if there was something missing for them like there had been for me, and sure enough, *this was the missing piece.*

I found that 60 percent of my clients were unhappy in their personal lives for one reason or another. I started diving in to find the source of the problem. We often worked on relationship stuff instead of business, sometimes for the majority of the time. We uncovered issues such as:

- Their significant other wasn't supportive of them building their own business.

- They were told they "Can't" do the things that would produce results, such as getting a new website, attending a mastermind retreat, traveling, or outsourcing.

- They were being forced to look for a JOB, since their business wasn't producing consistent cash flow.

- They were being talked down to: "No one is going to pay you to do that!"

- They had simply lost love for their partner and were living like roommates, without passion and intimacy.

- Some had no love life and didn't think they should focus on finding someone because they were too strapped for cash. How could they spend time on that when they needed to build their business and make money?

I could go on and on, but this is what I discovered during those deeper discussions with my clients.

I determined that I needed to help my entrepreneurs with more than just building and growing their businesses; I needed to help them with what I call "the love side" of their lives, too, because it all has to flow together. That's when I came up with the phrase for my networking: I help entrepreneurs get more love in their lives and money in their businesses. The two areas of life must go hand-in-hand in order for entrepreneurs to become fully successful, I think, and in order for them to live their happiest lives ever. That's what I want for you, for myself, and for everyone I meet.

If you're finally ready to break the cycle of unfulfilling or drama-filled relationships and either truly transform the relationships you have now or find new ones, then I say LET'S DO THIS!

If you're not satisfied with where you are right now in your love life, then why not see if my advice can help you? If you *think you're good* right now in your love life, I encourage you to make sure you're not settling. I've seen this over and over again with my clients when we really dive into what's going on with them in their personal lives. Together, we've been able to identify and resolve problems whose solutions have led to a tremendous increase in their level of happiness. So, read this with an open heart.

But first, we must evaluate our own level of self-love. Love for ourselves is the first thing we have to get comfortable with. I don't think there is anyone I've ever met, entrepreneur or not, who doesn't feel some level of discomfort with him- or herself. Do you truly love yourself? Do you believe that you deserve the most amazing love relationship that you can imagine? Do you realize that your love life could be the thing that's messing up your plan to develop a more successful and profitable business? *It could be.*

It's an amazing feeling to be in a truly love-filled relationship with someone who is 100% completely supportive of what you do and who doesn't question whether you know what you're doing or whether you are doing the right things. It can help you bring in MANY more clients and increase cash flow, too, when you have someone like that in your corner cheering you on!

Having an amazing husband like I do now is one of the single best things that I have going for me. It allows me to be more confident in what I'm doing, and it allows me to be proud and bold with the decisions I make in order to grow my business every year.

When I was single and dating, I longed for a loving relationship like this. It was on my mind pretty much every day, which affected my ability to really work my business the way it needed to be worked. I wasn't as motivated, I wasn't as confident, and I wasn't taking the action steps I needed to take on a regular basis, because I wasn't fully happy.

By Katrina Sawa

I believe to the core of my being that when we love ourselves, and when others around us fully love and support us, that is when we are able to pour our best selves into our families, our clients, and out into the world.

Here are a few tips for Making Your Love Life a Priority:

Just like you learn effective communication strategies in business, such as how to talk to your customers and prospects and model their ways of learning, you want to learn effective communication for your relationships, too.

In his book, *The 5 Love Languages*, Gary Chapman talks about how to express heartfelt commitment to your mate. The way you like to give or receive love could be completely different from the way your partner likes to receive it from or give it to you.

What is/are your love language(s)? You could have more than one. Here are three questions to ask yourself in order to find out:

1. What does your significant other do or fail to do that hurts you most deeply? (The opposite of this could be your Love Language.)

2. What have you most often requested of your significant other? (That thing is probably what would make you feel most loved.)

3. In what way do you regularly express love to your significant other? (What you do for them could indicate what you prefer to receive.)

Another one of my favorite relationship book authors is John Gray, who wrote the *Men Are from Mars* series. If you want to improve the communication or passion in your relationship, you should read his books, too.

Love is a choice you make every day. Your self-worth often depends on whether you are loved enough. Your business success depends on your self-worth.

If you want more love, you have to give it to yourself first, then to others. If the ones you want to love you can't reciprocate or won't work on finding out how to fulfill your love needs, then you have to think about what you want your life to look like moving forward and make a decision to stay and settle or move on and thrive.

It's obvious that communication is the key to building or rebuilding any new or existing relationship. However, both parties need to want to make it work if it's going to work. Both parties must also make an effort if it's going to work; wanting is not enough.

Through my numerous coaching calls with clients who were experiencing many of these relationship issues, **I developed a few lists of advice which I put**

into my book, *Love Yourself Successful*, and I'm going to gift you a digital copy of that book so you have access to those lists. Go online right now to www.JumpstartYourBizNow.com/JumpstartLove and get access. On top of learning how to love yourself more, and how to love what you're doing for your career or business, you'll get:

- My list of 6 Relationship Rescue types of activities and a worksheet designed to help you in your current relationship, or even in dating situations if you're single.

- My 8-Step action plan for working on or repairing your current relationship.

- My five-step action plan for letting go of the relationship(s) that isn't serving you any longer, because life is too short to settle.

Please don't settle for good enough: you deserve more!

About Katrina Sawa

Katrina is the creator of The Jumpstart Your Marketing & Sales System as CEO of Jumpstart Your Biz Now, CEO of Jumpstart Publishing, and an International Best-Selling author of *Jumpstart Your New Business Now, Love Yourself Successful, and 20 other books.* She's been featured on the Oprah and Friends XMRadio Network, ABC, and TheCW. Katrina loves to inspire and educate entrepreneurs on how to create a consistent money-making business doing what they love.

Jumpstart Your Money Vibe

4 Steps to Dramatically Shifting Your Personal Financial Energy

By Jackie Woodside, CPC, MSW

Recently, I was on a podcast with a gal from Canada named Brittany. Within seconds of meeting one another, we related as if we were best friends. There was an immediate connection. You have probably had that experience dozens of times. What is that?

It is the vibratory pattern of Brittany's inner world, matching that of mine. We share similar values, beliefs, interests, and paradigms about life and the world. We have a very similar "vibe."

Nikola Tesla, a Croatian American electrical engineer, once wrote, "If you want to understand the secrets of the universe, think in terms of energy, frequency, and vibration."

There is now proven data and science behind this notion of vibration and how it impacts your life. How you think, feel, what you believe, and your attitudes create a vibratory pattern that can be measured.

Scientific American published an article in 2018 titled "The Hippies Were Right! It Is All About Vibrations, Man." You can get hooked up to an electroencephalogram or electro magnetogram, and technicians can see the vibratory pattern produced by your thoughts and emotions.

Everything is energy. Simply put, everything is made of molecules, and molecules vibrate. A rock has a different vibration than a piece of paper. The same is true of human beings. People have different "vibes" according to their consciousness.

So, what's a Money Vibe?

The concept of 'Money Vibe' isn't just about dollars and cents, but an intricate weave of emotional, mental, and energetic relationships we all have with money.

When it comes to the inner game of money and success, your Beliefs, Emotions, Attitudes, and Thoughts—or BEAT for short—create the energetic vibrations that give rise to your habits, behaviors, relationships, and conversations, thus creating your life experience. We have lived with the false notion that we are the passive recipients of our thoughts and feelings, but nothing could be further from the truth.

To start understanding the concept of Money Vibe, call to mind an instance when you thought about or had a conversation about money. How did you feel? What did you think? What did you say?

Most people are filled with anxious, scarcity-laden thoughts about money. "I don't have enough. How can I get more?"

Those thoughts and feelings create your "Money Vibe." When you have a "low" money vibe, your beliefs, emotions, attitudes, and thoughts about money range from scarcity to anxiety and fear. The subsequent experience is that of lack, struggle, and uncertainty.

By bringing the essential skill of awareness to your inner world of experience, you can learn to direct your thoughts in a powerful, intentional, and creative way. Train yourself to use your mind in a new and different way, which leads to different thought patterns and new levels of confidence and decision-making.

Changing your vibe changes everything. And changing your Money Vibe will change your financial future.

Characteristics of High-Vibe and Low-Vibe People:

High-vibe people share several qualities:

- Happy

- Confident

- Optimistic

- Solution-oriented

- Calm, peaceful, centered

- Grateful

And high vibe people have different beliefs about money and success, such as:

- Things will work out.

- Money is everywhere.

- It's easy to make money once I get clear on my path.

- I can trust myself (and others) when it comes to money.

- I am optimistic about my financial future.

Low vibe people share these qualities:

- Anxious

- Stressed

- Worried about money, regardless of their level of income.

- Pessimistic

- Focused on problems, real or imagined

- Frustrated

People with low Money Vibe carry beliefs such as:

- It takes a lot of work to make money.

- I can't get ahead.

- I'm not one of the lucky ones.

- I can't trust myself (or others) regarding money.

If you find yourself located in the low Money Vibe range, don't fret.

First of all, it's not your fault. Secondly, and most importantly, you can change your Money Vibe, just like you work to strengthen a muscle or learn a new skill.

It's not your fault.

Human beings have an innate tendency to worry and watch out for what's wrong or what might harm us. It's something that social scientists and neurologists call the "negativity bias." Negativity bias is our natural tendency to see what's not working, what's missing, or what could go wrong as a natural instinct. It has been an evolutionary impulse since the hunter and gatherer days. Those who were happy-go-lucky out in the wilderness, not worried about what might come their way, made great prey for lions, tigers, and bears!

It's essential to understand your tendency toward negative thinking in this light: an evolutionary survival impulse that you no longer need and that you can change. We must train our brains in order for us to thrive!

Here are 4 reasons why you want to devote yourself to changing your Money Vibe and becoming one of those happy, grateful, optimistic people:

1. **Happier people earn more money.** A research study published in the Proceedings of the National Academy of Sciences showed that adolescents and young adults who report higher life satisfaction and happiness levels earn significantly higher incomes later in life. Happier people tend to be more engaged at work, take less sick time, and are generally more solution-focused. Therefore, when new opportunities emerge in the workplace, happier people stand out to management as the "go-to" employees. Promotions mean raises, and raises mean more significant financial opportunities.

2. **Optimism leads to great financial success.** A study published in Harvard Business Review showed that optimistic people earn more money. A study by Dr. Martin Seligman from the University of Pennsylvania found that optimistic salespeople performed 56% better

than those who tested as more pessimistic. Also, a study by Michelle Gielan, a UPenn Positive Psychology researcher, showed that people who test high in optimism are 40% more likely to get a promotion over the next year, six times more likely to be highly engaged at work, and five times less likely to burn out than pessimists. That is a strong case for showing optimism's value in success and financial well-being.

3. **Gratitude leads to increased prosperity.** A paper published in the National Academy of Sciences showed that gratitude raises optimism and self-esteem, and highly positive people earn more money.

4. **Conversely, 70% of lottery winners end up broke!** It may seem counterintuitive that lottery winners often end up in different financial positions. Still, it makes perfect sense when you think about it from an energy and consciousness perspective. People who change their outer circumstances without changing their inner consciousness will recreate the same conditions that match their worldview and belief system.

You can change it!

Now that you fully understand the importance of living a high-vibe life and maintaining high Money

Vibe beliefs, take the crucial next step toward establishing how you raise your Money Vibe! It's simple, but not always easy. The task is to focus on changing your habitual patterns of thought (called neural pathways) in order to change your behavior and what you attract into your life.

To change your Money Vibe, try these 4 crucial steps:

1. **Practice the Three Blessings exercise:** Dr. Martin Seligman's research shows that one way to raise self-esteem and happiness is to do this simple daily exercise: Write down 3 good things that happened in the past day and examine what your selections say about you! Adding that second part of the exercise is a game-changer. It doesn't have to be anything outrageous or out-of-the-ordinary. It could be, "I enjoyed a healthy lunch today, and what that says about me is that I am caring for my body by nourishing it with good food." Or, "I spent time helping my neighbor, and what that says about me is that I care about others and I am generous with my time." Research shows that practicing this exercise just a few times a week for three weeks increases self-esteem over three months.

2. **Spend time with high-vibe people:** Another essential factor in raising your vibe is to avoid

people who are addicted to negativity. It is shown that, through mirror neurons in our brains, we often unconsciously take on the emotional state of people around us. Be mindful of who you spend time with and seek positive-minded people.

3. **Change your thinking with the 3C's:** A simple (but not easy) exercise to change your thinking uses the 3C's method. What that means is that you first "Catch" a negative thought (i.e., observe it through self-awareness), then you "Challenge" the negative thought by talking back to it with your higher mind. You can ask things like, "Is that true? Is that what I want in life? Is that thought supporting my success and happiness?" Then, "Change" the thought by simply replacing it with a more supportive, positive, and uplifting thought.

4. **Use positive self-talk:** Positive self-talk is a powerful tool for managing low vibe thinking and emotions. Positive self-talk improves mood, increases happiness, builds resilience, reduces stress, boosts confidence, and helps to reframe negative experiences and view them in a more positive light. Talk to yourself like an uplifting coach or mentor, unlike the harsh inner critic you've developed thanks to our human evolution.

Our inner world of consciousness drives the results in our lives. I've spent years gaining experience in this realm and developing proven strategies to nuance the subtleties of how your beliefs, emotions, attitudes, and thoughts about money directly influence your financial reality. It isn't always an easy journey. However, I've had to overcome many obstacles myself: homelessness, domestic violence, chronic depression, addictions, and post-traumatic stress, just to name a few! Despite these challenges, or maybe because of them, I've helped thousands of people change their perspectives and Money Vibes so they were able to go on to live extremely prosperous and happy lives—and I want that for you, too!

If you're ready to take the first steps into shifting your personal Money Vibe, then I have a few free gifts for you. Just go to www.JackieWoodside.com/jumpstart to claim them.

- First, you'll receive access to a fun, engaging, practical, and FREE method to practice the skills presented here: My 30-Day Money Vibe Challenge. It is an experiment for which you set an intention regarding how much unexpected income you will bring into your life over the 30-day challenge. Then, you'll be guided by me with daily email messages to practice these skills (in less than 10 minutes a day). You will quickly see how changing your inner world impacts your outer experience!

- Second, you'll receive access to a training video called the 5E Formula for Financial Freedom, which highlights these teachings in more detail.

- Thirdly, and most importantly, if you want more support through your self-development journey, you'll be able to connect with me personally.

Thank you for going on this journey with me! I hope to see you inside the challenge!

About Jackie Woodside

Jackie Woodside is a USA TODAY and four-time Amazon bestselling author, TEDx speaker, international trainer, and professional coach. She is the founder of the Curriculum for Conscious Living and the Conscious Living Summit, and trains coaches around the world to deliver this life-changing work. Jackie has been featured on television shows with Jack Canfield and Don Miguel Ruiz, and educational summits with Marianne Williamson, Michael Beckwith, and Daniel Siegel. Her expertise is widely sought after as a teacher and speaker.

Jumpstart Your Personal Success

7 Simple Strategies to Achieve Any Goal

By Tiffany K. Martin

The demands of day-to-day life often require us to serve in various roles throughout the day. Working professional, entrepreneur, parent, spouse/partner, caregiver, domestic engineer, pet wrangler...you name it, conquering the daily grind requires us to pivot from one role to the next, often without transition or a break in between.

As we continue to keep up with the world around us, surviving our day-to-day, let alone thriving in it, becomes more of a challenge. How we show up is essential to the success and achievement of our goals. Whether pursuing our careers, taking care of others, cultivating self-care practices, or managing daily tasks, how we approach the journey impacts our destination.

Mother. Wife. Daughter. Health Advocate. Entrepreneur. Dog Mom. Mentor. Athlete. On any given day, these are the roles I play, fulfilling multiple roles on a daily basis. Each role comes with its own relationships and responsibilities, thus requiring me to show up differently for each one. I am often asked how I balance it all, and to be honest, I don't. It's not a matter of balance, but a matter of engagement—how I engage with others and how I engage myself. Life is hard, and being responsible for others is even harder. But having clarity on what you want to achieve, knowing the value it brings, and having a plan of action is the key to success. My objective is not to achieve balance between these roles, but to efficiently shift from one to the other and effectively achieve the objectives of each role.

Over the years, I have learned and developed simple strategies that will lay the foundation for success. These strategies can be applied to both life and work pursuits, and they will put you on the path to getting the most out of your endeavors. As part of your performance toolkit, these strategies will enhance your personal success by providing structure, increasing efficiency, moving you closer to your desired outcomes, and optimizing your results.

So, what do *you* want to accomplish?

1. Be S.M.A.R.T. About Your Goals

Most of us are acquainted with the idea of a S.M.A.R.T. goal. S.M.A.R.T. goals are: Specific, Measurable, Achievable, Realistic and/or Relevant, Time-Based.

Having a framework for your endeavors is the first step. Be specific about what you want to accomplish and realistic in defining the goal. Make sure that achieving the goal will influence your desired outcomes. Identify metrics or milestones that will allow you to measure progress and ensure your outcomes are achieved. Finally, don't fall victim to the "Well, whenever I get it done" mindset—pick a date for your goal and strive to meet it. Enhance your goal-achieving potential by writing down your S.M.A.R.T. goal. Goal-setting statistics indicate that if you write down your goals, you are 42 percent more likely to achieve them.

A clearly defined (S.M.A.R.T.) goal that is written down is the first step in personal success.

2. Identify the Root of Your Why

Now that you've defined your goal, ask yourself, "How will the achievement of this goal impact my life or work?" It's not enough to set a goal; you have to get in touch with the deeper reason for the goal by defining a Core Objective. Your Core Objective is the root of your goal, and it should be a clear and honest statement about the value added in accomplishing the goal.

Quite simply, your Core Objective is a deeper awareness of what you want to get out of achieving the goal. There have been numerous studies conducted on goal setting, and studies show that, **when it comes to goal purposes, those who have a deeper understanding of them have a better chance of achieving their objectives.** By identifying your Core Objective, the impact of achieving (or not achieving) the goal resonates more deeply and the goal becomes personal. By making the goal personal, you create a lifeline that brings you back to the root of your why.

When you find yourself lacking motivation or clarity, tap into your why and reflect how achieving your goal will be of value to you.

3. Release That Which Does Not Serve You

How you operate may be a function of what you think you should do, what you think others expect of you, or how you've been conditioned. Often, we do things out of habit or routine, and rarely do we question whether or not our actions and pursuits meet our needs or are in our best interest.

If you find yourself questioning what you're doing or how you're doing it, I invite you to reframe your approach. Before you act, ask yourself, "How does this serve me?" Over time, things and people change (including ourselves), and your previous means and methods may no longer be in alignment with your objectives. Just as a business reevaluates its operational plan, you too should evaluate how you operate. When you ask yourself the question, answer honestly. Remember your Core Objective: are your actions moving you closer to it? Are the tools, resources, and people in your life contributing to its achievement?

If things, people, places, and systems do not align with your Core Objectives, then let them go. Don't spend time dealing with something that doesn't get you closer to your desired outcomes.

4. Act With Purpose

It's not enough to do; you have to act with a purpose. Intentionality is the key to success, so focus on what you want, and be strategic in how to get it. Being intentional is active, not passive. Instead of just going with the flow, before you begin, think about how you want to end and proactively define a targeted outcome.

In all that you do, whether the task is big or small, think, speak, and act with intention so your outcomes can produce specific results.

5. Invest Your Time

Have you ever stated, "I don't have time for that!" or "Let me see if I can make time for that." Well, the hard truth is that you *do* have time to (insert said thing here), however, you have chosen to spend your time doing something else.

Just like money, time can be wasted, spent, or invested. I challenge you to be intentional about your time and do more than just spend it: invest it. Invest your time doing things that produce positive yields, fulfill you, or move you closer to your desired outcomes. If something or someone is important to you, schedule time for it, or them, and keep the appointment for yourself. You wouldn't miss a work meeting or an appointment, so be just as dedicated to yourself as you are to others. Remember, time is a non-renewable resource, and you never know how much of it you ultimately have left.

Be mindful of the time you have and make the most out of it by investing it in activities that have a direct impact on what you get out of life or work.

6. Show Up Ready

You know what they say: *Don't get ready, stay ready!* Your presence (i.e., how you functionally show up) influences what you achieve. As it relates to accomplishing tasks, be mindful of your physicality (Are you tired? Or dressed appropriately?), your mentality (Are you focused, clear-headed, and possessing the mental bandwidth to dedicate to the task?), and your emotional state of being (Are you centered, in control, and in the right mindset?).

When in pursuit of a goal, plan in advance and do whatever you need to in order to show up as your best self. Go to bed early. Eat healthily. Meditate. Wear your power suit. Get a haircut. Practice, research, or review materials. Use gear, equipment, or props. Listen to your theme song. Say your affirmations. It doesn't matter, just do you!

Preparing in advance and having a plan before you engage will contribute to you showing up as your best self and optimizing your results.

7. Manage Your Energy

If you find yourself consistently exhausted at the end of your day, despite your rest schedule, you may have an energy management issue. Your energy is your source, and you have to be intentional about investing it and protecting it. As opposed to approaching matters with the mindset that you'll give 100% or 110%, approach matters with the energy needed to accomplish the goal. Quality versus effort is not one-for-one. Some people can give 100% and produce low-quality results, while others can give only 60% and produce top-notch results.

Give what's needed without excessive over-giving. You do yourself (and others) a disservice if you consistently deplete your energy and end your day without enough energy for the people/activities that are important to you.

Assess what it takes to accomplish your objective and learn how to moderate your energy accordingly.

BONUS: Things to Keep in Mind

We've covered some simple but effective strategies that can be applied to life, work, projects, and endeavors. As you continue your journey and move toward achieving your desired outcomes, here are a few things to be mindful of:

- **Mindset + Action = Results:** It's not enough to have an action plan; you also need a behavioral plan. How you do is often more important than what you do. Identify the thoughts and behaviors that promote successful action.

- **You Always Have a Choice:** Your attitude, how you spend your time, and what you choose to sacrifice are all choices. Even when you feel your choices are limited or unreasonable, the choice is still yours to make. Be mindful of the outcomes your choices will have on moving you toward your goals.

- **It's Never Too Late to Begin Anew:** You are never really starting over; you are starting anew. You carry the lessons learned from past endeavors, and the knowledge you gain is never lost. You can always step away, reset, refocus, come back to, or let go of a goal—it's never too late to redefine your course in life.

The final step is to put the strategies into action. It's not enough to have strategies; you must take action, apply those strategies, and continue to learn and evolve along the way.

Your personal toolkit has been upgraded with new strategies, and you are ready to Jumpstart Your Personal Success! **If you want to go deeper, execute with more intention, and optimize your goals and results, I'm here for it! As a gift to my readers, I am offering you the following FREE resources to get started today:**

- **Define Your Core Objectives Worksheet** to help you craft your Root Goal Statement

- **Mindset & Behaviors Assessment** to make the shift from limiting to achieving

- **Time To Take Action Plan** to help you move closer toward your goal

- **Daily Intention Sheet** to set and track your intentions for each day

- **Get Started Video** where I step through each of the resources to help you start strong

You can get access to all of this and more online at www.TKMartinConsulting.com/jumpstart. I can't wait to work with you! #PlanExecuteSucceedRepeat

About Tiffany K. Martin

Tiffany K. Martin is the Owner of TKMartin Consulting LLC. Serving as a Performance Coach and Change Strategist, Tiffany is a thought leader with expertise in Personal Performance, Diversity, Equity, Inclusion & Belonging (DEIB), Strategy Development, and Change Management. Tiffany provides clients with the strategies needed to achieve their goals efficiently and successfully. It is her passion to share her knowledge and experiences to help others become better and do better.

Jumpstart
Your Business
Chapters

Jumpstart Your Book

The Magic is in the Rewrite

By Tom Pfeifer

I was riding the bus with my friend Jenn awhile back, and we were talking about our work passions. She said she admired my ability to write. To paraphrase:

"I like to write. But it never comes out well." This is one of the primary reasons people give for not writing regularly or proficiently.

I replied to Jenn with my favorite quote from Pulitzer Prize-winning author James A. Michener: "I'm not a very good writer, but I'm an excellent rewriter."

Jenn jumped on the concept and now she not only likes to write, but she also uses this secret to make sure her ideas come across clearly without a wasted word. It's why, I believe, she has climbed the corporate ladder at every company for which she has worked, and why she is now a senior director at a national recruitment company.

Becoming (in fact, being) a writer is a process. It's a journey. You take away as much as you put into it. A professional writer writes virtually every day. Most follow a set schedule.

I have known I wanted to be a writer since I was seven years old. I was the original geek. I majored in journalism in college—not because I intended to become a journalist, but because it was the only hands-on writing curriculum offered. I didn't want to learn *about* writing, I wanted *to* write. Besides, I reckoned, Mark Twain and Ernest Hemingway had been journalists, so it must be good training.

After I graduated from college, I spent 15 years as a journalist, fine-tuning my writing skills under some phenomenal mentors. I wrote my first book while working as a congressional communications director, writing 15 minutes each morning before starting my 12- to 20-hour days. But I never published any of it. I was 62 before I wrote—and published—my first book.

Over the years, I have learned what has worked and what hasn't. One of the most important lessons I've learned is that you must write if you are going to get better at it. No matter what your skill level, you can— and will—get better. And, once you reach the next skill level, you can—and will—get better. And, once you reach the *next* skill level, you can—and will—get better.

It's a never-ending process. If you want to be a better writer, you must write. Period.

Every professional writer I know is also an excellent rewriter. It's what separates professionals from amateurs.

And it works whether you're writing the great American novel, a non-fiction book, or a TEDx speech. As an example, in what I can only describe as an uplifting New Year's Eve message, I received the following email on a particular December 31st:

> *Hi Tom,*
>
> *Quick note to share that I just finished reading your book. I'm preparing to present at TEDx URI later in February, and my mom gave me a copy of your book to help me prepare. Timely, pertinent, practical, it put me at ease that my writing, rewriting, rewriting, and rewriting was not only normal, but necessary and part of the hard work necessary to do an excellent job. Thanks for the wisdom and insights.*
>
> *~Pete*

When I posted the message on LinkedIn, I learned from a production services manager at a major U.S. bank that the book Pete cited, *Write It, Speak It: Writing a Speech They'll APPLAUD!* is used in the bank's public speaking training sessions, too.

Now, I have never met Pete, nor his mom, as far as I know. Nor had I ever met the production services manager. It's one thing when friends and family praise your work—you usually expect that. It's a whole new ballgame when strangers validate what you do.

And the validation comes from the fact that I rewrite virtually everything I draft before releasing it to the public. Because *it's the rewrite that results in magic.*

Here are my three golden rules to rewriting any piece you may write:

> 1) Write, then rewrite, and, if necessary, rewrite again.
>
> 2) Print it out and read it aloud. Then rewrite.
>
> 3) Have someone with good editing skills look it over. If necessary, rewrite again.

Why rewrite? Susan M. Tiberghien spells it out in *One Year to a Writing Life: Twelve Lessons to Deepen Every Writer's Art and Craft:*

By Tom Pfeifer

When asked about rewriting, Ernest Hemingway said that he rewrote the ending to *A Farewell to Arms* thirty-nine times before he was satisfied. Vladimir Nabokov wrote that spontaneous eloquence seemed like a miracle and that he rewrote every word he ever published, and often several times. And Mark Strand, former poet laureate, says that each of his poems sometimes goes through forty to fifty drafts before it is finished.

A professional writer is their own harshest critic and most meticulous editor. Sure, there will be others to critique and edit your work, but it starts with the writer—and it starts with rewriting.

Rewriting is another word for self-editing and is an integral part of the writing process. With each rewrite, a piece becomes clearer, more concise, more colorful, and more professional.

Rewriting also cures writer's block. Rewriters are not concerned about quality in any first draft. They expect it to be horrible. Often, it's just a free-flow exercise of getting ideas down. Writing without worrying about professional standards is an extremely liberating concept. Only through rewriting—or self-editing—does a piece take shape. Sculpting the phrasing and placement, moving paragraphs, finding just the right adjective, adverb, and verb—that's the fun part of writing.

Content vs. Copy

Editing, or rewriting, comes in two flavors: content editing and copy editing. The process is the same whether done by the rewriter or a separate editor.

Editing for content is the first and, some argue, the most important editing process. It is also the most stimulating. It is during this process when you fill in the holes.

- Does the piece grab the reader?

- Do the ideas flow in logical sequence?

- Are they comprehensive and comprehensible?

- Is there a beginning, middle, and end in a storytelling narrative?

- Does the news release or business letter answer the who, what, when, where, and why questions?

- Does the business letter get to the point in the first paragraph?

- Is the media release or news story written in inverted pyramid style?

- Will the target audience understand what you have written, or does it contain jargon that needs to be explained or reworded?

- Is it funny—intentionally?

- In fiction, do the characters maintain a consistent point of view and act within their characterization?

A thorough content edit may take three, four, five, or 39 more edits to ready a piece for publication, depending on the length of the piece and the skill of the writer. (The more skilled the writer, the more rewrites a piece will endure.)

Don't let this hold you back though! You don't have to be a good writer to write your own book. You can get your ideas out on paper, or even talk them out, then ask a professional to help you finesse it into a very good book. You can do this!

There is no set rule for how many rewrites a piece should go through. I rewrite until I'm satisfied that a piece of written work is the best it can be—or until a deadline forces me to push the "Send" button. I've written pieces with which I was satisfied after the first rewrite. But unless I'm posting to Facebook or Twitter, that's rare. (Yes, I do edit my posts before I post.) For short pieces of 1,000 words or less, most of what I write goes through a minimum of three rewrites before I think I'm done.

A rewrite could be as simple as tightening up some sentences. It could be as involved as moving some paragraphs around for better flow. Sometimes I've found the nut (the theme or main point) buried within the piece and rewritten it with the nut as my lead. And that doesn't count the partial rewrites I do within a piece as I'm writing it.

Once, I wrote an 800-word column for a newspaper that went through several massive rewrites. After the first write-through, I realized I needed more research to plug in. I found it and plugged it in. There was still a hole in the flow. I researched some more and added the new information to the mixture. Then I moved words, sentences, and paragraphs around, deleted some now-superfluous material, and massaged it until it felt and read right. Like I said, you don't have to do this yourself if you aren't experienced with the process.

Once I thought I was finished, I printed out the piece and read it aloud. Words are meant to be spoken. You'll find typos, dropped words, and flow problems while reading a piece aloud. Oral reading always leads to a stronger piece.

Content editing is followed by copy editing. A copy editor reads over the copy line by line in search of grammatical and spelling errors. Such edits include ensuring the correct "there," "their," or "they're" is used; that "it's" is used in place of "it is" and not the possessive "its"; that the semicolon is not misused; and that the Oxford comma is used—or not used—consistently. A copy editor may also edit for content, but that is not their primary objective. I can assist my clients with any and all of these services, depending on their expertise and abilities. I love fine-tuning any written piece, article, post, or book!

Once the writer has self-edited until satisfied the piece is ready for publication, he or she hands it off to another editor. A separate pair of eyes is critical to catching the holes in logic and grammatical errors you've read over and over again without seeing. In our own work, we see what we know we meant. But by rewriting and rewriting until the piece is nearly professional, the errors caught by the outside editor are fewer—and the editing costs are lower.

I have twin daughters who have edited my writing from the time they were eleven years old until they moved out of the house. They loved finding the errors of their daddy's ways. If you don't have children, find someone else to edit your drafts. If the first person you pick doesn't find errors in at least two out of every three pieces you write, then find someone else. Because you will make errors you don't see, no matter how many times you review it.

Writing, rewriting, reading out loud, and giving your work to an editor may not make you a James Michener. But, like Jenn, you will be significantly more satisfied with your writing. Then, when someone compliments your writing skills while complaining about their own, you can smile and say,

"I'm not a very good writer, either. But I'm an excellent rewriter."

Because *it's the Rewrite that Results in Magic!*

Do you want to be an excellent rewriter? Do you have a book in you? Want to improve your writing for many purposes? I'd like to gift you a free white paper on all you need to know to write a book, including structuring your book, finding the time to write, and how to use stories to bring your points home.

Simply go to www.JumpstartYourBook.net now and get access to this. In addition, you'll have the opportunity for a 30-minute free consultation with me. When you mention this chapter on our call, it could earn you five hours of free coaching — a $3,000 value!

Here's to jumpstarting yourself as an author to increase your authority!

About Tom Pfeifer

After 15 years as a journalist and 15 years on Capitol Hill as a congressman's mouthpiece, Tom Pfeifer founded Consistent Voice Communications. He is the author of *Write It, Speak It: Writing a Speech They'll Applaud*, and in 2022, he earned his World Class Speaking Coach certification. Tom coaches people and groups on book writing and speechwriting. He helps clients to determine the right niche for their books or keynotes, and guides them through the writing process.

Jumpstart Your Business Growth

The 3 Non-Negotiable Business Foundations

By Christine Campbell Rapin

Business growth can be elegantly simple, yet many solopreneurs struggle to achieve business success.

The biggest challenge is that many new business owners lack the business skills and a solid understanding of the business foundations that are needed to create repeatable success. They simply launch their business with a dream of creating an impact, together with time and financial freedom, only to realize they have created an expensive hobby and not a viable business.

I began my first business in 2018 as a side hustle, working an hour a day alongside my corporate career and family life. Having spent over 25 years in the world of business, working across industries, in different parts of the world, in a mix of roles including marketing, sales, and operations, all while having profit and loss responsibility and leading teams, I knew what I needed to focus on to create consistent client growth.

The results I was able to create in those short periods of time gained attention from my peers, especially those who were struggling to gain traction with clients. This led to invitations for coffee, during which my acquaintances picked my brain about what exactly I was focused on.

The roadmap I shared was simple: I treated my business like a business.

I was hyper-focused on the 3 building blocks that fuel business growth for any business, regardless of its size, industry, or business foundation (solopreneur or enterprise). **I call them the three non-negotiable business foundations:**

1. Building an audience of buyers who are problem-aware and actively looking for support to achieve their desired results.

2. Mastering my marketing message to spark curiosity about my services so I can predictably create movement that will shift someone from simple curiosity to becoming a paid client.

3. Creating and presenting offers whereby the value and predictability of achieving the results by working with me is higher than working the problem(s) on their own.

This elegantly simple formula is the key to building a strong foundation for business growth and scalability. It is the foundation I've created and implemented with more than 400 businesses to achieve more than a billion dollars in combined revenue.

If you are looking to jumpstart your business growth, get out of overwhelm, and create a profitable business that you own instead of one that owns you, this chapter is for you. These are the three non-negotiable business foundations that every business needs to see consistent business growth.

Let's begin with the first non-negotiable business foundation that all business owners need to understand: Building Your Audience of Buyers.

There are two actions that will predict your future revenue:

1. How many people are you meeting who are problem-aware and who may need your services—or who can connect you to your ideal client?

2. How many offers are you making to people who are problem-aware and who are actively

prioritizing and seeking support to achieve their desired results?

Simply put, your business will be built on strangers. Building a strong pipeline of potential clients is the single biggest predictor of whether you will create momentum and results as a business owner. That is why, if business growth is your goal, these two actions need to be your primary focus. Everything else is busy work that is distracting you from creating client growth traction.

Building an audience of buyers requires an intentional strategy that enables you to stand out from the sea of sameness. To do this effectively, you must develop a deep understanding of the desires, aspirations, motivations, and choices that create movement with your ideal client.

An elegantly simple way to think about your audience is to view them as being in three lanes of traffic: the slow, middle, and fast lanes.

In the slow lane, your ideal client may have some awareness of the problem for which you present a solution; however, they do not view this as a current problem for them specifically. Consequently, there is zero motivation or urgency to take action today. Getting out of this lane, or limiting your focus on educating this group, is essential if you want to create consistent client growth, because these people are not yet buyers.

In the middle lane, your ideal client is aware there is a problem and has likely experienced this problem more than once. When the problem arises, they generally ride through the rough patch without seeking support or intervention to change the inputs that create the problematic experience. Therefore, the pattern repeats. When they reach the point where the consequences of the problem become unbearable, they realize a change is needed. If you can identify when that moment occurs, focus your marketing efforts at the place where you can disrupt the pattern, and offer to guide the prospective client to an alternate path to create a different result, then you can identify a potential buyer.

In the fast lane, your ideal client is aware of the problem and highly motivated to seek external help to achieve the desired results, because they recognize they can't get there on their own in the timeline they need. They have committed financial resources and have a timeline for getting started working with an expert. If you are visible and well-positioned as the "must-hire expert" to help them achieve their desired results, and you make a compelling offer where the value of the results is exponentially more than the investment of your services, they will commit to investing and moving forward. This is what we at CLEAR Acceleration Inc. call the unicorn client: a highly motived buyer. The more effectively and consistently your marketing and sales strategy is executed, the more unicorn clients your business will attract.

Understanding and applying this simple analogy of the three lanes of traffic will help you to prioritize more effectively who you are investing your time nurturing. Each lane requires different strategies and tactics, and flexing your approach will make your sales and marketing efforts more effective.

You might be wondering, what marketing strategies and tactics should I be using for each lane?

There are thousands of strategies and tactics that will create results. The key is to determine which ones will resonate with your ideal client and suit the way in which you want to grow your business.

A simple way to approach this question is to evaluate what 20% of your efforts are creating 80% of the movement in your business right now, and use the Pareto Principle to step out of marketing overwhelm. Choose your lane and commit to mastering the skills to be even more effective at those particular strategies. From there, as you improve your proficiency, you will want to establish structures in your business to support this framework. This is how you can scale your business without working 24/7 or living in overwhelm, always chasing the next shiny object.

For example, one of my clients who runs a digital marketing agency business focuses primarily on networking and SEO in their marketing strategy. They see really great results when they take the right actions consistently in those areas, and they can avoid almost all other strategies completely. You don't have to do it all!

My *main marketing strategies to attract mentoring clients* are speaking and networking events. I love being part of experiences where I can build relationships with fellow business owners, and I find that filling my own sales pipeline this way maximizes my time and attracts 90% of the right types of clients.

Note that the need to attract an audience of buyers never stops.

Audience building is essential, because only 3% of potential clients are ready to purchase in any given day. You need to be nurturing the other 97% and consistently focus on creating movement through messaging that helps people transfer from the slow lane to the fast lane with predictable outcomes. We advise our clients that, even when you are already experiencing consistent client growth and have low capacity to onboard new clients, you still need to commit 50% of your day to building an audience of buyers. If you are looking to scale or grow, then 70-80% of your effort needs to be focused on new client attraction in order to build momentum.

Positioning yourself as the "must-hire expert" is the key to the second non-negotiable business foundation. Every business owner needs to learn to master their marketing message.

Marketing can feel overwhelming or be viewed as a necessary evil to many new or struggling business owners because we take a haphazard approach without really understanding the simple purpose behind all marketing efforts.

Regardless of the tactic chosen, marketing has one elegantly simple goal: to move your potential client from simply being curious to becoming a paid client with predictable results.

Conversations with your ideal client will bring real-time insights and provide you with critical feedback that allows you to evaluate whether your messaging is having the desired effect of creating movement—or whether it needs adjustment. Only once you have mastered your messaging should you consider adding an accelerator such as investing in paid advertising. Before that happens, you are throwing money away because you are unlikely to see a strong ROI that creates repeatable results.

A great free resource for learning to improve your messaging is our podcast, "Amplify Your Marketing Message with Christine Campbell Rapin." We talk about various tactics to build an audience of buyers and how to effectively move people from curious audience members to paid clients.

This leads to the third non-negotiable business foundation, the all-important offer.

To have high client conversion rates, your offer must be viewed by your potential buyer as a pathway to creating predictable results that are highly valued by your ideal client. Only when they view you as the "must-hire expert" who will guide them to achieve their desired results more quickly, with fewer resources and less effort than they are currently applying on their own, will they be willing to invest in your offer.

When you can confidently communicate and build trust, prove that you know how to achieve the results, and demonstrate that you have the right skills, capability, and compassion to be the right guide to help your ideal client achieve their desired results, your business growth will accelerate.

Business growth can be elegantly simple when you understand the three non-negotiable business foundations. Helping service-based businesses to build this roadmap is what I do. **I invite you to visit my website at www.ChristineCampbellRapin.com/jumpstart for a few free resources to get you started today!** When you do, you'll receive five, short 20-minute training videos and a one-hour webinar on How to

Scale & Attract High Paying Clients Without Complicated Tech. These resources are curated to help you accelerate the growth of your business and build the three business foundations for scalable growth. Get Clear. Become the Must-Hire Expert. See Results.

About Christine Campbell Rapin

Christine Campbell Rapin is a business mentor and consultant. As the owner of CLEAR Acceleration Inc., she has a no-nonsense approach to helping business owners achieve consistent client growth by improving client conversion rates. Creative service-based business owners seek her out to create consistently profitable businesses by implementing effective marketing and sales strategies to scale to multiple six figures without working 24/7.

Jumpstart Your Customer Experience

5 Keys to Creating Loyal Fans

By Katrina Sawa

Have you ever experienced such horrible customer service that it drove you to Yelp to write a scathing review? How about the opposite? Do you go to the same lengths when the customer service is at a five-star level? I've written both types of reviews. I've also experienced both situations in my own business. Luckily, I can count the number of bad experiences on one hand, and the good are too many to count. When you're a solopreneur wearing all the hats, it's not easy to do it all. Things do slip through the cracks due to lack of time, or as a result of simply not knowing what's missing.

I've had my own business now for 21 years, and there have definitely been very hard times and huge learning curves. There have been more pros than cons for me, however, because now I am enjoying the fruits of my efforts and the wisdom gained through trial and error. But it took me a while to get there.

Whether you're thinking about starting a business, you already have one, or you work for a company, I think it's important to concern yourself with what kind of customer experience you provide. Is it memorable and favorable, insignificant and neutral, or detrimental and lackluster?

Just as you evaluate the service and experience you receive as a customer at the hundreds of establishments or companies you frequent in a month, a quarter, or a year, your customers and prospects are doing the same.

And how exactly can you tell what kind of customer experience or service you or your company are providing? Yelp reviews? Customer testimonials? Feedback via posts or likes on social media? We definitely know when something goes awry, since most customers will report that. We don't always know when our customers have a favorable or even a WOW experience. Some will go out of their way to share that positive experience, but many won't.

So, how can we make sure our customers not only have a memorable and favorable experience using our products, services, and programs, but that they have a WOW experience?

By Katrina Sawa

This year was the year I was going to turn a big focus on taking steps toward providing a WOW customer experience. I listened to podcasts, speakers, and trainings, I asked friends and peers, and I watched how companies interacted with me. Did they think of all the tiny details I typically watch for? Did they correspond enough but not too much? Did they forget about me after a week, a month, or more? Did they make it easy to buy, to get information, to find out more? Could I actually see who was behind the business? I don't trust a website that doesn't show me at least the owner's name, photo, and location. I also hired more advisors, copywriters, and team members to support my efforts; *I'm no longer going this alone.*

Those are the things I've been looking at within my own business. My hope is that, with this information, you can review your own customer journey, processes, and correspondence to see what can be enhanced.

Our customers are the lifeblood of our business. We have to continually get better at finding and supporting new customers with our marketing and sales efforts, of course. But in addition, as a business owner, if you are *not* marketing to those people who already know you or have done business with you in the past, *you are missing out on a lot of repeat sales and trusted referrals.* I see too many entrepreneurs focusing more on the acquisition of new customers than nurturing current customers. That's a big mistake; you have to focus on both.

When you are in that first meeting with a new prospect (whether in person or through your website), **you need to *get them curious, make them want more,* and *feed them all the information they could ever possibly want,* or they may go elsewhere.** Now, that doesn't mean you blurt out everything and anything about your business in one sitting or on one page. However:

- If they have to search for something, then we're not doing a good enough job.

- If they have to ask questions, then we're not doing a good enough job.

- If they wonder what we're offering/selling, then we're not doing a good enough job.

- If they can't find things like refund policies, full contact info, or even how to make a purchase, then we're not doing a good enough job—and they're going elsewhere.

After working with thousands of businesses over 25 years, let me share what I believe will help you create a WOW Customer Experience.

1. **Provide Ample Info** – Providing information with enough detail and in various modalities for all the different learning styles your customers may have, is key. Too many online

marketers try to get fancy with funnels, but with barely any information on their landing pages. They think the simple salesy headline, one or two sentences or bullets of info, and an urgency to buy or sign up will work. It does for some people, like the bigger known industry celebrities. But for the majority of folks, it's just not enough information for someone who's never heard of you to make a buying or opting in decision, in my opinion. It could work on men more than women, since men generally like things simple and women tend to buy more on emotion. In addition, customers want to hear about updates to your products and services without necessarily receiving a sales pitch.

2. **Make Them Feel Good** – Customers want to feel welcome and comfortable from the get-go and throughout your relationship with them. Some people or websites make you feel inadequate, lost, incapable, unaccepted, or left out. How do you think that results in your customers feeling about you? Instead, you want to make them feel worthy, proud, confident, and good about themselves. You can hit their hot buttons and pain points without shaming them. You want them to feel like you're being honest with them, so there are no surprises later. It's also important to

understand their needs and expectations so you can build systems to support them.

3. **Look the Part** – If you want people to believe that you are the expert and they should hire you over someone else, then you need to look like an expert—in person, virtually, and on your website. Have professional photos, caring, heartfelt video messages, glowing testimonials, memorable branding, and unique selling proposition. Don't talk too much about yourself, however, at least not right off the bat. Talk about them and their needs, wants, challenges, and desires. You have to look good, but don't make it all about you; that will turn some people off right away.

4. **Create Loyal Fans** – We've all heard the saying, "They have to like, trust, and connect with you before they're going to buy (or be interested in more)." So, how do we do that? How do we create fans, not just subscribers or followers? Here are a few ways I think you could enhance your Fan Factor:

   a. **Add more videos** on your website that feature you speaking directly to your ideal client; talk to ONE person. They need to feel your energy, hear your passion, and connect with you. On almost every page of your website, you could add a video sharing about the page they're on, what they might be looking for, how to navigate their problem, and what to do. Videos are also helpful for sharing your story, purpose, personality, values, and philosophies. Many people won't buy until they learn what matters to you and how you align with them.

b. **Ask questions** of your customers and website visitors. Have them take a quiz, assessment, survey, or simply fill in a form to get access or learn more. Via email, you can ask them to reply and share their ideas, comments, and feedback. Some people will love knowing that you want to learn more about them.

c. **Leverage technology** for enhanced customer experiences. Knowing how to automate a few key areas of their journey will help you keep in touch with a lot more people than if you try doing it all one by one.

d. **Create a customer-centered culture** where they come first. Offer ways to reach you 24/7, even if the connection is automated. Have more than one way they can get in touch; don't be afraid of giving out your address or phone number. And think of outside-the-box ways to thank them.

5. **Be Consistent** – Do you follow through, follow up, and walk your talk? Are you being consistent with your message, promise, brand, expectations, and authenticity? Or do you switch gears as soon as they sign up or buy? Can they rely on your content, products, and services, or are you all marketing fluff and no real meat? Do you continually attempt to serve them at the highest level, or are they forgotten after time?

Business is *not all about list building*. That's a big part of it, because it's true: ***it is a numbers game***. The more people you get in front of, people who will read/watch your content every month, the more opportunities you will have to get more clients.

It's also about retention and referrals. If you don't WOW your customers right from the beginning and they don't continue experiencing love from you on a regular basis, they could very well go elsewhere. What you're saying in those emails, posts, videos, calls, and podcasts matters. If you don't know how to word things right, you may not see traction or gain raving fans who continue to refer you year after year.

If you are frustrated with the lack of sales or referrals to your business, or you want to get a new business started the right way from the beginning, then I've got some free resources on a special page just for you. Go to www.JumpstartYourBizNow.com/wow now and you'll get access to:

- **A free video training** on all 8 aspects of running a consistently profitable business. Entrepreneurs often miss 2-3 of these, as they get too busy and aren't good at prioritizing.

- **My Need Number Worksheet**, which will help you determine your true money goals. Most Entrepreneurs set goals that are too low and unrealistic to their basic needs plus "want" needs.

- **An outline and instructions on how and what to delegate** or outsource in your business, and when. It's vital that you start building a team sooner than you think.

Paying attention to your customer experience and all the possible little details on their journey will serve you in the long run, so go see what tweaks and changes you can make today—and reach out for support. I'm here to be a resource, confidant, and mentor.

About Katrina Sawa

Katrina is an International Award-Winning Speaker and Author with 22 books. Entrepreneurs hire her to learn exactly what to do and how to grow their businesses quickly. Katrina is passionate about finding the holes and opportunities for business owners to monetize and systematize so they can work less and make more. Katrina hosts numerous trainings, mastermind retreats, summits, and one-on-one coaching to help others get a jumpstart—fast!

Jumpstart Your Message

Your Message Matters and Can Make a Difference

By Arvee Robinson

You have a message to share that only you can share with people who can only hear it from you. That message will save someone's business, life, or even their soul. I used to think that, if you couldn't deliver your message, it would be taken away from you and given to someone else.

Then one day, I was sitting in church and the priest said, "God has given you all unique gifts, unique meaning one-of-a-kind. If you don't use those gifts, they will be unused for all eternity." In that moment, I thought, "That's it! That's the same as your message!" If you don't deliver your message, it will be undelivered for all eternity. Consequently, those people whose lives you were supposed to save will go on suffering. That is why it is so important for you to share your message with the world.

You may be thinking, "Okay, how do I do that?"

Using the acronym MATTERS, here are seven ways to jumpstart your message:

M stands for Millions. Once perfected, you can deliver your message to millions of people, over and over. There is no limit as to the reach of your message; the only limit is in your own mind, your level of willingness to step outside your comfort zone. You can also make millions of dollars by selling your products, services, and ideas from the platform. All you need to do is to develop your million-dollar message.

A stands for Audience. For the best results, speak to groups with your target market and your ideal clients in the audience. Keep in mind that audiences have changed over the years. Listeners no longer tolerate long, boring speeches. They want concise, honest, and to-the-point communication. Every decade, audiences change their preferences about what they want from a speaker. In the 70s, audiences tolerated lectures. In the 80s, they wanted more of a presentation. The 90s were all about conversation, and we just left the decade of experiential speaking, where audiences wanted to be a part of the presentation. Today, audiences are searching for what I call *naked authenticity*. This means they are looking for speakers to be real, to be vulnerable, and to be who they truly are. The greater the authenticity, the greater the impact.

T stands for Training. Before you step on stage, get professionally trained as a speaker. There is no such thing as a natural born speaker, only trained ones. Take as many public speaking training courses as you can find, hire a public speaking coach, and learn the right way to develop and deliver your message.

T stands for Truth. When you are speaking on stage, you become the authority on that topic. As the authority, people in your audience will automatically believe you. It is important to speak the truth and nothing but the truth, no matter what. If you don't, it could backfire. There might be someone in your audience who is an expert on your topic. Or, if you leave out too much of the truth, people may fill in the blanks and make up something that is worse.

When I was six months old, I had pneumonia and it settled in my ears, causing severe hearing loss. At school, I would play and talk to my friends while the teacher was teaching. Written on every report card was the same message: "Arvee talks too much!" Little did they know it was because I couldn't hear and I was asking my friends, "What did she say? What are we supposed to do?" My hearing loss went undetected until I was thirteen. Finally, one of my teachers sent me to get a hearing test. My parents were surprised at my low test score; they thought I just didn't listen. They immediately took me to an ear specialist who scheduled my first operation, a stapedectomy. In simple terms, they replaced one of my inner ear bones with a tiny wire. This changed my world forever. I could hear!

When I was sixteen, I was scheduled for my second ear surgery, only this time, I was embarrassed to tell my friends. So, I lied instead. I said I was going into the hospital for some tests, and I would be absent for three days. When I returned to school, to my horror, it was rumored that I'd had an abortion. This was impossible, because I was a young woman of faith and a virgin. In that moment I realized that, if you don't tell the truth, people will make up their own truth—and it won't be pretty, it will be ugly. Don't be afraid to share the truth.

E stands for Evolution. Your message will evolve over time. You will also evolve as a speaker. The fastest way to accomplish this is to get started. Once you are trained, share your message with whomever will listen. Take massive action and sign up for as many speaking engagements as you can find. It is all about stage time. The more stage time you have, the faster you will evolve into the speaker you want to become. One day, you will realize that you are changing lives with your words.

R stands for Rehearse. To be the best speaker you can be and deliver your million-dollar message, you need to rehearse—and rehearse often. As a matter of fact, you need to practice your speech for one hour per two minutes of speech. That means, for a 30-minute presentation, you will need to practice for 15 hours. That's what it takes to be good. If you want to be a great speaker, you will want to rehearse twice as long. Rehearse your speech so much that you become the script. Know it forward and backward. Be the speech, and you will be able to add a story or anecdote whenever you feel that someone in the audience needs to hear it. It's true freedom on stage.

S stands for Stories. Stories are the most powerful presentation technique you can use. Everyone loves a good story. Stories act as invisible selling tools. Stories open the hearts of your listeners, who then open their pocketbooks. There are three stories you must have in your presentation. The first one is your professional story. This is the story about you and how you got into the business you are in. Your professional story earns you the right to speak about your topic and gives you instant credibility. Only share in your story what is relevant to your speaking topic. There is no need to share your entire life story. Also, the stage is not a place for healing from past wounds. Be sure to heal offstage, then bring your story onstage and heal others.

The next important story to add to your speech is a success story. This is typically a testimonial about someone who has worked with you and, as a result, they are enjoying great success. For example, one of my clients, Hector, dreamed of teaching the Hispanic market how to make more sales and increase the quality of their lives. Hector thought that, just because he had a voice, he could go out and speak without being properly trained. He failed miserably. No one bought his products or services. Realizing he needed help closing with prospective clients, he hired me as his coach. I saw what he was doing wrong, he corrected it, and the next time he spoke, he closed $4,500 in sales. Now, he has those skills for the rest of his life. Another story you need is a story with a lesson. Typically, you don't share the lesson with your audience; instead, you let them find the lesson on their own.

Years ago, I was a mentor for the Billionaire Adventure Club, and we went to Egypt. As a group, we decided to visit the great pyramids of Giza. At the time, I thought walking into a pyramid would be like walking into the Luxor Hotel in Las Vegas. You walk in, look around at the artifacts, and leave. I was mistaken. We all had to bend down to fit into the small entry and then walk on a wobbly slatted wooden board down to the center of the pyramid.

As we walked in, hunched over, the light from outside suddenly went out. Panic-stricken, I turned for a quick getaway. The guy behind me said, "Are you sure?" In my mind, I had been thinking, *I'll come back to Egypt and do this at another time.* After hearing his words, though, I knew I would never come back, and this was my only opportunity to see inside this great mausoleum. I turned back around and continued my journey downward. Once inside, there was nothing to see except an empty crypt. I came, I saw, and I bolted out of there. As I was leaving through the narrow, dark path, a woman from our group was coming from the opposite direction toward me. She was 6 feet tall and blocked the passageway. She asked me to take her picture and handed me her iPhone. Now, she knew good and well that we are not supposed to take pictures inside of the pyramid. However, she was the only thing between me and the doorway. I grabbed her phone, clicked the picture, and ran past her.

For the past two decades, as a public speaking coach, I've been teaching others how to jumpstart their message, speak on stage, sell from the platform, and change lives for a living. I host virtual and in-person workshops, run group programs, and offer online courses you can take if you want to use speaking to grow your business (or if you want speaking to BE your business).

My students tell me they love my step-by-step speaker system. One client even said, "Your system is powerful and easy to use. When I have to give a speech, I just pull out your system, follow it step by step, and voila! I have a persuasive presentation that I know will move people to action." I'd love to help you, too!

If you would like to learn more about how to jumpstart your message, which will help you with speaking, and how public speaking will help grow your business fast, I invite you access a few powerful resources online at www.ArveeRobinson.com/jumpstart.

On that page, you'll have access to free trainings, videos, and more, including a private strategy session with me during which I will teach you how to create your own public speaking money-making strategy.

The world is waiting for your message; it's time to share it.

About Arvee Robinson

Arvee Robinson is The Master Speaker Trainer, international keynote speaker, and three-time bestselling author. For two decades, she has taught business owners how to use public speaking as a marketing strategy so they can attract more clients, generate unlimited leads, grow their businesses fast, and make a difference with their words. She has trained over 5,000 individuals and given over 3,500 speeches globally, sharing the stage with many speaking giants.

Jumpstart Your Network

3 Essential Steps for Earning More with Referrals

By Virginia Muzquiz

Nine out of ten business owners say they rely on referrals to generate revenue for their businesses. *Fewer than one in ten have a plan to make it happen.*

If you're one of those without a plan, then you've just hit the jackpot, because I'm about to hand you that plan! And when you implement it, you'll land among the top 3% of entrepreneurs who consistently earn six figures AND have the financial freedom and leisure time to live the lives they intended to have when they got into business in the first place!

I developed this system in the early 2000's when a local education franchise hired me to sell tutoring to families with children in urban schools in our area under a government program called No Child Left Behind. In just under 6 years, we grew from $0 to $2.5 million in annual revenue—completely by word of mouth!

Now, for more than a decade, I've been helping entrepreneurs just like you generate consistent revenue by referral, without complicated marketing funnels, confusing tech, or budget-busting paid traffic. If you are looking for a way to add $100K or more to your business and live your life by design, read on!

It is the mindset shift that jumpstarts referrals.

I have found that the vast majority of entrepreneurs know they need to network. And they do. They bounce from event to event to event, trying to find clients. But their efforts are to no avail. They tell me they are exhausted, overworked, and underpaid for their efforts. That's because, at any given time, only 3% of your *ideal clients* have buying urgency. So, even if you were networking in a room of 100 of your ideal clients (which almost never happens), only 3 of them are looking for someone like you! And if there are more "yous" than just you in the room—well, your odds of finding a client just got worse!

The solution to this conundrum is to STOP networking for clients and START networking for partners who have influence with your ideal prospects and who support them in ways you don't. For example: I teach a powerful form of client acquisition. My accountant partner sees people's numbers. She knows whether a client is onboarding a steady stream of clients or not, and she refers the ones who are networking ad nauseum and struggling to meet their revenue goals to me.

In turn, when I speak with clients who have started making more money, I refer them to my accountant to start making sure their money is all going in the right buckets, and that they're maximizing their larger incomes accordingly, etc.

Referral marketing is a win-win-win for everyone involved.

This single shift in perspective has provided many of my clients with MASSIVE increases in revenue (one of my clients increased their revenue by 372%!) and dramatically more free time. Imagine getting three times the income in a third of the time you are currently spending on networking! What would your life look like?

The Referral Alchemy® Secret

Step 1: Connect

Connecting means creating an opportunity to initiate potentially beneficial relationships. It's about networking with the *right* people, because not all connections have the resources, experience, and networks that complement your business well enough to help you grow your income and free up your time. Here are some simple steps you can take to ensure you are connecting with the right people:

1. **Define your TRIBE.** Who do you most want to serve? Most entrepreneurs hate the idea of narrowing their focus because they think it will shrink their opportunity to find a client. Nothing could be further from the truth. If you want a partner to find your ideal prospects, they need to know what they are looking for! Without a clear picture of who you want as a customer, your partners won't know how to find you a solid prospect.

2. **Become a TRUSTED AUTHORITY.** I cannot count the number of times I've heard an entrepreneur say: *I just can't seem to explain to people what I do so they understand it and want to work with me.* I hate to say it, but that way of communicating is a HUGE problem. Your prospects won't hear a word you say if you don't speak their language, and they won't care what you do or how you do it. They want two things: empathy and results. So, make sure your messaging acknowledges their pain and paints a picture of the outcomes they most want. How you get them there is far less relevant than you think.

3. **Design your TEAM:** Stop networking with everyone and start focusing on connecting with people with whom you want to do business and who will support your ideal prospects in ways you don't. Who are those people? Make a list. Having trouble? Ask your past and existing clients what other kinds of services related to your industry they invest in. Dr. Greg, a physical therapist who implemented the Referral Alchemy® System, focused on connecting with chiropractors, personal trainers, and energy healers. Within one year, he increased his revenue from $67K a year (barely scraping by) to $262K a year, which allowed him to hire a receptionist and a part-time therapist. In doing that, he increased his book of business while decreasing his personal workload, which allowed him to pursue his hobbies and spend more time with his wife.

Step 2: Curate

Think of this process kind of like a draft for a sports team. Just because someone is a catcher or a first baseman, doesn't mean they are a good fit for the team. They need to have the right skills and the right attitude to play on *your* team. What are some things you might want to consider as you field your team?

1. Do you share a similar mission, vision, purpose, and values? People who believe in

your mission, support your vision, share your purpose, and align with your values are more likely to bring you great prospects than those who do not.

2. Are you impressed by their work and level of professionalism? It's essential that you find them to be referrable, because your referral partners will expect reciprocity.

3. Do they have resources, knowledge, and networks that would be beneficial to your personal and professional growth? And do you have resources, knowledge, and networks that would benefit them? Again, reciprocity is a key element of creating profitable business relationships.

4. Are they givers? Far too many of the people who hire me do so because they feel like they are giving abundantly, but not getting anything in return. Beware of the takers and stop giving as soon as you realize they are not going to reciprocate!

5. Are they consummate connectors? About 80% of the networkers we meet are what I call *algorithmic* networkers. Basically, they will respond "yes" or "no" when we ask if they know someone, but that's as far as it goes. About 16% of networkers are *archaeologists*. They will take a look in their contacts to see if they

are connected to the kind of people you need to know. Finally, about 4% of networkers are *alchemists.* These are the people who have enough influence to use their connections to make connections that benefit you. Your goal is to build your team with as many archeologists and alchemists as possible.

Step 3: Collaborate

One of the tragic mistakes networkers make that costs them time, money, and often their dreams is spending too much of their time and investing too many of their resources and connections *too soon,* before a solid relationship has been established. Instead, I teach my clients to build a NEXUS: a team of professionals that actively promote, connect and refer them regularly, by specific agreement. That way, they can do the right work with the right people at the right time. Here's a quick overview of the system we use:

1. When we meet a new person for the first time and collect their contact information, we classify them as an ACQUAINTANCE. The *only* step we take with an acquaintance is to schedule a "getting-to-know-you" meeting. The goal of the meeting is to learn about the potential referral source and confirm whether they are a good fit for our NEXUS (the part of our network that actually *works* for us).

2. After this meeting, we move our acquaintance to ASSOCIATE status. At this level of relationship, we are still not offering support, resources, or connections. If we see that there might be synergy between us, we make an offer of another meeting where we can talk about how we might support each other's business goals.

3. The purpose of this next meeting is to discuss what resources, knowledge, and connections we have to share and to create a plan for *promoting* one another. At this point we are just looking for ways to make one another *visible* to our respective audiences. For example, we might choose to do a webinar swap, invite each other to be guests on our respective podcasts, or share some social media posts. Notice that we are not making client referrals yet. At this level of relationship, we classify our referral source as an ADVOCATE.

4. When we discover that we not only have similar audiences, but we also know potential referral partners for one another and actively make *connections*, we add to the promotional strategies a plan for connecting one another to the business professionals we know who might become part of our NEXUS. We call these partners AMBASSADORS.

5. Finally, there are those partners who are having regular sales conversations with potential prospects. Even the best sales professional can't close every prospect. Your ALLIES are able to turn a *no* for them into a potential *yes* for you. These partners not only promote you and connect you to potential NEXUS partners, but they also regularly send you prospects that are ready to sign on the dotted line. These partners are truly few and far between, but when you cultivate and nurture 3-5 of them, your business will thrive.

If you truly want your networking to make you money, then consider putting this plan in place! I've put together some valuable resources to help you with this process.

1. The Referral Alchemy® Report reveals the #1 secret most gurus don't talk about and why it's holding back your marketing efforts, how to triple your clients in one-third of the time, and the single most powerful action you can take NOW to activate your network and achieve your goals.

2. The Referral Alchemy® Roadmap eCourse (delivered via email over 2 weeks) will walk you step by step through my proven 3T system for turning your networking into a powerful marketing strategy that is guaranteed to

dramatically increase your influence, your income, and your impact.

3. Complementary access to my Get Connected® Bootcamp online training that reveals how to leverage the science of reciprocity, network with the right people to get results, and build a six-figure referral NEXUS that brings you referrals—on demand! Plus, I want to be sure that you can implement all you learn without getting stuck or derailed, so I'm including 30 days of unlimited laser coaching with your Bootcamp enrollment so you can get all your questions answered!

You can access them all at www.MasterConnectors.com/jumpstart today and get started earning more by working less!

About Virginia Muzquiz

Virginia Muzquiz is the founder of Master Connectors, Inc. and the creator of the Referral Alchemy® which teaches coaches, consultants, and experts how to turn their networks into referral-generating machines. She is passionate about increasing prosperity across the globe and uses her business to further the efforts of Ten By Three, an international non-profit that creates economies of scale in Third World countries by turning artisans into entrepreneurs. Virginia lives with her husband, Victor, in O'Fallon IL, and when she's not teaching you can find her enjoying time with her daughters, wrestling with her grandson, or traveling the globe!

Jumpstart Your Sales

One-on-One Sales Conversation Mastery

By Katrina Sawa

Are you excited about making more money in your business or career? If not, why not?

Money allows you to do whatever you want to do, and it also allows you to serve at a much higher level. Money helps you create your dream life, invest in your future, donate to good causes, and cover family expenses beyond the day-to-day, such as college, home down payments, vacations, retirement, paying down debt, and so much more.

My goal with this chapter is to get you excited about making more money, and then give you some tips on how to do that. First, however, you will need to *want* to make more money; it's not enough to get excited about it. You won't do the things necessary to make it happen if you don't truly *want* it.

So, why should you want to bring in more money?

Think about it this way:

If you *had* to create $10,000 in 30 Days, what would be your plan?

If your kid, parent, spouse, or loved one suddenly needed a necessary, life-saving surgery that cost $10,000, how would you create those funds if you didn't have them in savings or on a credit card?

Those circumstances might ignite a fire under you to go make money or sales, wouldn't it? In my case, eleven years ago I was told I needed two total hip replacements. They wouldn't do them together; that would've been too hard on me. But I did need to have them pretty close together. So, I scheduled one for January and the other for December of the same year. I had plenty of time to recover in between, and I could basically buy one and get one "free" with my insurance deductibles. However, because of the extraneous expenses from that year and the lost revenues due to my inability to travel and speak, coupled with my lack of stamina for some other revenue-generating activities...I pretty much just brought in the basics that year. The following year, the bills had added up so much that I was forced into bankruptcy.

Quickly after that, I ramped my business back up and once again I had reserves because, thankfully, I knew how to make money: I knew how to sell effectively. If you plopped me in a city where I knew no one and there was no internet, I would know how to go get clients and make sales. Would you? *Without the internet?*

Whether you're an entrepreneur, a sales associate, or an employee, you can always affect your moneymaking ability. And you can't rely on social media or the internet for sales; it's just too busy. That doesn't mean sales won't come from there, but you still have to master your sales and selling ability.

Making more money and jumpstarting your sales requires three things:

1. The confidence to go after what you want.

2. The opportunities available to you.

3. The skills to know how to do it, whatever *it* is.

I'm sharing more about selling in one's business, but you can apply much of this to other jobs where you have to do your own client generation, or even the sales and closing strategies with your children and family! Generally, I'm talking about selling one-to-one here, although of course you can sell from the stage or through a virtual event as a speaker, and you can generate sales from people who land on your website. But where you'll sell tens of thousands of dollars consistently will most likely be in one-on-one sales conversations.

In order to Jumpstart Your Sales Conversations, you will need to hone your skills and business strategies around the following four areas:

1. **Fill your calendar with sales calls and appointments.** Do you know how to do that, or do you have effective systems for people to get on your calendar virtually? If you have to touch and correspond with each and every lead or prospect who comes your way, you won't be talking with enough people. It's a numbers game, it always has been. And now, more than ever, with the expansive number of places online where your prospects are looking daily, you have to hook them in wherever they see you or find you. You have to have amazing systems in place and attention-grabbing copy or wording to make them stop and pay attention. Then, you have to hold their attention long enough and get them curious enough to want to know more. You have to make it easy for them to sign up to talk with you. In my experience, having reviewed thousands of entrepreneurs' websites and lead generation processes, the majority of people do not do this well enough to be effective.

2. **Know how to dance in those conversations with objections, questions about pricing, and incentives to take action today.** You can't be afraid to share the reasons why someone should work with you or buy your product. You can't be afraid to ask them if they're ready to sign up, or if they have any more questions before signing up. You want to be comfortable talking about money, their money, and how they can find the resources to invest. You don't want to be stuck without an answer or a response to whatever concerns they may have. Being prepared with the answer to any question or situation is key. Having bonuses or incentives are a great way to get prospective clients to commit today rather than "think about it," especially if the offers are juicy enough. Try using bonuses before discounts—although discounts work well, too. Give a time limit for them to decide before the discount or bonus is gone. See what happens!

3. **Be assertive and consultative, not salesy and sleazy, and remember to ask them to take the next step.** Be curious and interested in solving their problem. Ask questions of them to build rapport and trust so they feel like you understand them. I even share tips I've shared with others if a certain topic comes up; I don't hold back all my ideas. I want to make them

aware that I already have a plan for growing their business quickly. Once they say yes, I even get them started on their next steps right then and there; I don't make them wait.

4. **Have the right offerings and business models, or know how to develop custom packages on the fly.** Know your limits for pricing, the lowest you can go, or what you can throw in for bonuses to get someone to act today. Start with your highest offerings that are a good fit, then go down from there. Don't start low and go up—that never works! Have a way for someone to try you out if they aren't willing to go all in with a larger or longer package. I offer a three- or four-call package if someone is interested but not quite ready to dive into my six-month or annual program just yet. Have a way to take the money today, too, even if you make up a new package. Get the technology in place to make it easy for you to ask for their credit card on the spot; don't leave the sign up in their hands to be finalized in the follow-up.

Are you effective in the majority of your sales transactions and conversations now? Do you close the business, make the sale, or land the client in MOST instances? If not, it could be time you enlisted a script—or at least a list of questions to ask, points to cover, responses to common objections, and offers you can make. That's how I got started, and sometimes I still keep some notes handy.

Scripting is the best way to help you overcome some of the biggest frustrations in the sales process. This is why my coaching clients record me during our calls together. I'm very good with the words. They like to use my words and phrases during their sales conversations, and also in their emails, marketing materials, webpages, and videos.

Sales scripting can help you build trust easily, avoid losing sales by delivering options prematurely, and overcome anxiety or fear about what to say. It can ensure that your sales conversations always follow a persuasive sequence, steering a path to a strong close.

Here are my 5 Favorite Closing Techniques:

1. Optional Close – Give them choices, like: "Do you want this, or that? Six months, or a year? Start now, or in 30 days? Pay with PayPal, or with credit card?" Give them options instead of just "yes" or "no."

2. Assume the Sale – Assume they are going to buy, because why else would they come to a call with you—and be shocked if they tell you no.

3. Fear of Loss – Make them feel like they will really be missing out if they do not buy from

you. What would they do instead? This product or service is going away.

4. Sense of Urgency – Create a sense of urgency. Make them feel that they need to hurry up and buy before the product and/or service is gone, the price increases, bonuses go away, or because there's a limited quantity or seating available.

4. Indifference – Make them feel that it doesn't matter to you whether they buy or not. Explain that it's not a big deal and that it's up to them.

What else can I tell you in such a short chapter?

Get support and training when you want to learn more about sales and selling. I've had a handful of mentors on my entrepreneurial journey from whom I've learned techniques and strategies, including wording and effective phrasing. I've had to finesse all I've learned over time into a system that works for me and for the clients I serve. But I keep evolving that system, those words, as the marketplace changes and my offerings change along with it. Be open to the evolution of yourself and your business, your customers, marketing and sales strategies...all of it.

I invite you to visit my website for more tips and trainings centered around sales, marketing, and maximizing your website efficiency and systems to make all of this grow faster for you. Go to www.JumpstartYourBizNow.com/salesV6 and I'll see you over there! Don't be shy, reach out. If there's one thing I know about being good in sales, it's that you can't be too afraid or resistant to asking questions—which includes asking for help. We're all in this together!

About Katrina Sawa

Katrina is an International Award-Winning Speaker and Author with 22 books. Entrepreneurs hire her to learn exactly what to do and how to grow their businesses quickly. Katrina is passionate about finding the holes and opportunities for business owners to monetize and systematize so they can work less and make more. Katrina hosts numerous trainings, mastermind retreats, summits, and one-on-one coaching to help others get a jumpstart—fast!

Jumpstart Your Speaking Calendar

Practical Resources to Get You More Bookings

By Jackie Lapin

Smart marketers know that whatever business they're in, speaking can accelerate client attraction and growth.

Speaking live or virtually in front of an audience increases that Know/Like/Trust factor, which minimizes the barrier to enrollment or purchase. People who resonate with you will want more, and speaking in person just makes people WANT to have a relationship with you, once you've demonstrated the ability to solve their problem or advance their dreams.

Once you've established what you are offering and who you serve, then it's a matter of creating one or more signature presentations that first offer value and then provide a pathway to their "promised land."

Not everyone's path is to become a "keynote" speaker who is paid for their presentations. That is especially true today, when paid opportunities are fewer and pay less (ever since the pandemic). So, it truly behooves anyone who uses speaking for revenue to have three different speaking skills in their arsenal:

- Speaking to Enroll—A willingness to speak on stage (live or virtual) with the presentation ending in an offer of some product, coaching program, or other educational construct that provides forward motion for the prospective clients in the room.

- Speaking to Inspire Opt-In—A willingness to simply offer an irresistible free gift from the stage—a lead magnet—that compels people to opt-in digitally, so you can begin a relationship with them that may result in a future sale. This is required from stages that won't let you make a paid offer, but which allow you to collect emails.

- Speaking as a Keynoter—This is where you are paid for your presentation by an organizer who has a budget to bring in speakers for corporate, association, non-profit, or conference speaking opportunities.

You can always start with one presentation, but having three with different topics (or three that are slightly repackaged for different types of audiences you seek to woo) will give the booker more choices. If you have only one arrow in your quiver, it had better be a bullseye! But if you have three, you increase the likelihood of finding something that appeals to more bookers.

Your ultimate goal is to get in front of audiences comprised of your ideal clients—and the booker is the gatekeeper.

What motivates a booker to bring you on board is RELEVANCE!

So, what factors make you relevant?

- Your message is right for this demographic, age, gender, and mindset match.

- You solve a specific problem that challenges this particular audience (this is the single most important factor you can convey in all your booking materials and conversations).

- Your subject matter is compelling—there is some urgency implied, some need-to-know.

- You offer something unique, different—not run-of-the-mill.

- Your story is their story—you've been there yourself and can show them the way.

- Your topic is timely, current, and relevant to what is happening now.

- Your credentials and expertise are significant to this audience.

- You inspire and ignite the audience with specific practical steps or advice.

- You match the theme or subject matter that is pertinent to this group or event.

- You are the right skill level for this audience.

- You have authored a book that reinforces your authority.

- You have spoken at other meetings, venues, or events that also reinforce your authority and desirability.

- You are within the affordability range of the meeting/event's budget.

Why is this so important?

Because it will be the backbone of your proposal letter and your speaker one-sheet, two of the three tools you need when pitching yourself to a booker. You don't have to use all of these points of relevance, but being able to draw upon several will strengthen your case for getting booked.

To present yourself to a booker, you need to craft a proposal letter that's no more than about 7 paragraphs. It initially addresses why you would be a powerful speaker for this audience, what's the problem, and how does your presentation solve it. You can go on to recount your supporting credentials—the WHY YOU? part of the letter. And then, perhaps you can present some of the take-aways that the audience will experience upon hearing you. What will be the outcome? Lastly, ask either to be considered as a speaker or scheduled for a Zoom meeting to get better acquainted so you can explore how you might serve this organization. Keep it short and concise. And toward the end, advise them you have attached your speaker one-sheet and 3 to 5 minutes of video of you presenting, preferably on live stage—and if not, from a virtual stage.

So, let's talk about Speaker One-Sheets.

These are two-page, graphically appealing showcases that shine a light on you as a compelling speaker.

You can't put all of your information into a proposal letter, so the speaker one-sheet adds more depth to who you are and what you present. It features a bio on the front page that speaks to the problem you solve—along with a couple of testimonials, preferably from bookers who have previously had you on their stages. (Clients and people who have heard you speak will stand in until you get some great quotes from bookers.)

The back is devoted to your three presentations, featuring a little about each one. These two pages are illustrated with great images of you—a headshot, and perhaps one of you speaking—as well as book covers, logos of companies where you've presented or served, media who have interviewed or featured you, plus any awards you've been given. Most of all, it must look professionally designed. However, there are less expensive options than retaining a custom graphic designer.

Be prepared to fill out a lot of forms, too!

When it comes to meetings, associations, and other professional staging events that have multiple speakers, the materials we have discussed are most likely to be your way in the door. But many conferences today won't even give you the name of the event coordinator or meeting planner. Your only choice is to submit via online form—a Call for Speakers form. It behooves you to save time and duplication by creating a "cheat-sheet" with most of the elements that will be required (a long and a short bio to suit either request, a summary of your proposed presentation, your further credentials, etc.) Once you fill out a few, you'll get a sense of what these events are seeking in their Calls for Speakers.

What happens next?

Now you decide what types of opportunities you want to seek. If you are just starting out, speaking at local meetings is a great way to go. Once you are more experienced, you may want to speak to meetings, but farther from home. Today, with so many companies still holding virtual meetings, you can speak almost anywhere without leaving home. But live meetings have come back in a big way, and you need to decide how far afield you are willing travel.

You can start pursuing bigger events once you have a solid idea of how your presentation performs, and you've been building your confidence and mastered your stage presence. These larger events include conferences, associations, corporations, events hosted by other industry pros, and trade shows.

Where does your audience hang out? You may be looking at a variety of other types of opportunities—for example, special interest groups (parenting, seniors, health and wellness support groups, military, LGBTQ, ethnic, etc.). Perhaps you're a good fit for spiritual or faith-based venues or organizations, addiction recovery centers, or yoga centers. Or maybe your topics apply to job placement programs, civic or service groups, etc. Look for places where your audience congregates.

Where/how do you find them?

This is a no-Google bashing zone! Yes, Google is actually your very best source to zero in on those ideal venues. Use key words for your subject matter and meetings, or add in your city to find them. You can also use Google to find conferences: subject matter + conference.

Other great sources are Meetup and Eventbrite, as these now feature recurring meetings, not just one-time events. Looking for associations? Search for the Directory of Associations. Want a look at upcoming conferences? Search for Events in America.

Now, there are some great shortcuts available from SpeakerTunity®, The Speaker & Leader Resource Company. You can obtain one of 75 regional directories or 60 niche specialty directories with meetings all across North America, just in your niche. SpeakerTunity® Conference Connections is a subscription service that gives you access to 4,000 events per month that are seeking Calls for Speakers—they've pulled them all into one place.

You've got your tools, you've got your leads. They only thing left is to actually start pitching yourself. But here's a tip! Most people never get around to doing this work when they think they will. Life gets in the way. I recommend you block off a minimum of three hours a week on your calendar for booking outreach. Or retain/train someone to do it for you. Otherwise, your powerful message and the gift you have to offer to people who need you will be dormant.

I hope you're inspired to get out there and speak more, either in person or online. **I want to give you some resources to make this much easier for you.**

Go to www.SpeakerTunity.com/jumpstart and get access to the following gifts from me, just for you, because you're reading this chapter:

- One month FREE of SpeakerTunity® Members Only!

- A free cheat sheet to help you write snappy, irresistible speaker presentation titles that will get you booked.

- A discount to get YOUR OWN speaker one-sheet done for you.

- Multiple opportunities to speak or learn about other resources via our regular emails.

These should give you a great JUMPSTART.

Now, go out and get booked!

You deserve to be seen, heard, and hired!

About Jackie Lapin

Jackie Lapin is the Founder of SpeakerTunity®, The Speaker & Leader Resource Company with 75 speaker lead directories including TEDx. SpeakerTunity® provides leads, tools, and strategies for leaders, coaches, and entrepreneurs to get booked for speaking engagements, radio shows, podcasts, virtual summits, and more. With trained virtual assistants you can retain to do outreach for you, it's the Ultimate Speaker's Toolbox that will propel you onto more stages—faster!

What's Next?

What did you think of the stories and expertise that our authors had to share?

Did you learn a few new things to take back to your life or work?

My hope is that you did learn a few things, or at least walk away with a fresh new way of thinking about some of our topics. If so, please go over to Amazon and leave us a review! Make sure you choose the "teal" colored *Jumpstart Your* _____ book as there are five others there.

Our authors have been hand-selected due to their level of expertise, genuine integrity, and overall skill level in their industry. If you enjoyed reading some of their stories or learning more about how they help their clients, please take the next step and reach out to those who spoke to you.

Most of the authors in this book speak to groups of all sizes, both in person and virtually. They also offer products, programs, events, and services that can support you in one or more areas of your life, health, wealth, or business / career.

I highly recommend that you take advantage of their special offers, additional downloads, and more when you visit each of the websites listed at the end of their chapters.

In addition, I've put together ONE page on my website where you can access all of the Jumpstart Author's websites and special offers, to make it easy for you to follow up. **Go to www.JumpstartBookAuthors.com** right now, before you forget who you wanted to connect with or find out more about. All authors from all Jumpstart books are on that page.

Thank you for reading this book, and I look forward to bringing you more Jumpstart Authors in upcoming books, plus more training and teachings in my own books.

If you are an author who has something that YOU help people JUMPSTART and you would like to be considered as one of our next Jumpstart Authors, please go to www.BecomeAJumpstartAuthor.com now and apply!

WHAT DO YOU HELP YOUR CLIENTS JUMPSTART?

In the *Jumpstart Your* _____ book series, YOU Fill in the Blank with the thing YOU do with YOUR clients for YOUR chapter and become an author within a year! Use your book as a MARKETING TOOL to get leads and grow your business.

Interested in becoming an author easily?

Get into a compilation book of 10-20 authors and write ONE chapter, but get huge exposure for you and your business, along with every author promoting it alongside you! Attract new clients and make more money after your prospects are introduced to you in this book.

Want to get more exposure, speaking gigs, or clients in the coming year? Become an author!

While it could take a while for you to write your own full book, it's relatively easy to get published in an anthology or compilation book by just writing one chapter. Everyone in the book promotes the books and sells them, so you get in front of a lot more people than you would with just your own book. PLUS... we do all the work! **Find out how this could benefit you here: www.BecomeAJumpstartAuthor.com or go find out how to write your own full book, market your books, or just get help with certain aspects** of publishing. We offer A la Carte pricing. Info at www.JumpstartPublishing.net.

ABOUT KATRINA SAWA

CEO OF K. SAWA MARKETING INT'L INC., JUMPSTART PUBLISHING, AND JUMPSTARTYOURBIZNOW.COM

Katrina Sawa is known as the JumpStart Your Biz Coach because she lovingly kicks her clients and their businesses into high gear, online & offline, and fast. Katrina is the creator of the Jumpstart Your Marketing & Sales System, Jumpstart Your Business Cash Flow System, and various other online tutorials and trainings for entrepreneurs of all levels. She is an 13x International Best-Selling Author with 22 books and CEO of Jumpstart Publishing as well where she helps over 60 authors each year become authors and/or best-sellers.

Katrina's first, hosted anthology book, *Jumpstart Your* _____ (Yes, that's a blank.) was published in Fall of 2018 and now every year Kat gets to help 10-20 entrepreneurs become authors as a new volume is published annually.

Affordable Book Publishing Services & Consulting
www.JumpstartPublishing.net

Katrina helps entrepreneurs make smarter marketing and business decisions in order to create the life and business of your dreams. She helps you create your big picture vision, plan and initial offerings if you're just starting out. She helps you develop a more leveraged, efficient business and marketing plan if you're more seasoned. And she helps you implement more effective websites and online marketing opportunities. Either way, she shows you all the steps, systems and marketing that need to be put in place in order to accomplish your big picture business, life, and money goals. She does this via one-on-one coaching, various short, and longer-term group programs, her in person and virtual Jumpstart Events, Webinars, Podcasts, and even inside her Jumpstart Your Business & Marketing Facebook Group.

As an international speaker, Katrina won the National Collaborator of the Year Award by the Public Speakers Association of who's conference which Katrina spoke for four years in a row. She is also a member of the Women's Speaker Association, eWomenNetwork, Women's Prosperity Network, Innovation Women, Leap for Ladies, and a Diamond Member of Polka Dot Powerhouse. Kat speaks to groups and conferences of all sizes all over North America and the Internet.

One thing that makes Katrina different is that she also focuses on her clients' personal lives. She found that most business owners lack enough self-confidence to truly enable them to get to their next level, or take those leaps of faith they need to achieve their ultimate dreams. This is the primary reason wrote her book, *Love Yourself Successful* back in 2012 and then released a 2nd Edition in 2022. Katrina's goal is to inspire, motivate, and educate entrepreneurs on how to love themselves fully, live a bigger life, leverage themselves to complete happiness, and not settle for good enough, but go after their best life ever instead!

Katrina has a degree in Business Administration, Marketing Concentration, from California State University Sacramento, and has been a featured business expert on three of her local television news channels throughout her career thus far. She has also been featured in the Los Angeles Tribune, Comstock's Magazine, Lead Up for Women Magazine, Top Talent Magazine, and Amazing Women Magazine.

Katrina lives in Northern California with her husband Jason, stepdaughter Riley, and their dog Luna, where she enjoys glamping in their 33-foot travel trailer, traveling, entertaining and of course, wine!

You can find out all about Kat and her products, programs, services, and live events online at

www.JumpstartYourBizNow.com,
www.JumpstartEvents.net, and
www.JumpstartPublishing.net.

Why Work with Katrina?

Wouldn't it be great if you had the clarity to see beyond your blind spots?

Wouldn't it be great to know exactly what sets you apart and to know what to say to get more people to like, trust, and connect with you?

Being confident in what you offer and clear with what you're doing in your business is just the beginning. When you work with Kat, you get someone who works with you, side-by-side, helping you create everything from your strategic big picture plan all the way down to the nitty gritty of your day-to-day revenue generating activities.

Plus, Katrina makes sales and marketing fun! She shares how to become more efficient, productive, and effective with the right positioning, brand, messaging, offers, pricing, tech, tools, team, and more.

> "Katrina literally has SAVED ME months of trial-and-error time, as well as saved me incredible amounts of MONEY by avoiding costly mistakes."
>
> ~ *Sharon Marsh, Ph.D*

Learn more about coaching with Kat at www.JumpstartYourBizNow.com/coaching or schedule a Free Laser Coaching Call with her today at www.JumpstartYourBizNow.com/FreeCallWithKat and jump right in!

Jumpstart Resources

Motivate and Inspire Others!

"Share this Book"

Retail $18.95 + Tax & Shipping

Special Quantity Discounts

5 - 15 Books	$11.95 Each
16 - 30 Books	$9.95 Each
30 - 1,000 Books	$7.95 Each

To Place an Order Contact:

K. Sawa Marketing International Inc.

916-872-4000

info@JumpstartPublishing.net

or go to www.JumpstartPublishing.net

If you enjoyed this volume of Jumpstart Your _____, you will love the other 5 books in the series too. Go grab more!

There are six books total with 71 additional authors. You can read all of their stories, tips, and get their free gifts too.

Find them all on Amazon here:

https://www.amazon.com/dp/B083DM3BWY

Or at
www.JumpstartBookStore.com.

Grab One or More of the Free Jumpstart Your Business Trainings Now!

Learn How to:

- Get Started Speaking
- Jumpstart Your Business
- Implement Best Marketing Practices
- Build an Effective Website
- Create a Life You Love
- Find Your Purpose
- Love Yourself Successful
- Delegate & Build Your Team
- And more!

Get Access Online at:

www.JumpstartYourBizNow.com/FreeTrainings

Want a Deeper Training on How to Start, Grow, Market & Monetize Your Business?

Attend One of Kat's in Person & Virtual Events!

- In Depth Training, How-To, Templates

- Roadmap & Plan to Jumpstart Your Biz

- Hot Seat Coaching

- Learn from Topic Specific Speakers

- Mastermind & Network

- Make Money with Easy YES Offers

- Everything you need in one place

Get Information at
www.JumpstartEvents.net

Want to Become an Author or Learn how to Publish a Book?

Professional Book Writing and publishing is Easy if you know WHAT to do, WHERE to get stuff done, and HOW to publish, especially if you want to do it the most affordable way possible, yet still have a very professional looking book.

Do You Have a Draft, or an Idea for a Book but Don't Know How to Get It Done & Turn It Into a Real Book?

You may need:

- Support to finish and fine tune the manuscript

- A beautifully designed cover

- A great editor to make your book sing

- A marketing plan for book launch and sales

- A book webpage or author website

- And so much more…

Access a free training and info about publishing and becoming an author today, don't wait! Go to www.JumpstartPublishing.net.

Book Katrina to Speak:

Katrina Sawa is an International, Inspirational Speaker. A few of the topics of her presentations include:

- *Love Yourself Successful*
- *How to Make Fast Cash with Easy Yes Offers*
- *8 Secrets to a Consistent Moneymaking Business*
- *Marketing Basics for Consistent Cash Flow*
- *5 Ps to Bigger Sales Results*

"Katrina is a dynamic speaker, and she had the audience on the edge of their seats. In addition to learning some great marketing strategies they were truly enjoying themselves. I have seen Katrina speak on other occasions and what I love is that each time, I have a new "Ah-ha!" moment about how I can improve my business and marketing strategies."

– Tina Angell

Learn More About Booking Katrina at
www.JumpstartYourBizNow.com/speaking

Manufactured by Amazon.ca
Bolton, ON

35236163R00098